# AS Music Study Guide

**OCR**

Huw Ellis-Williams, Veronica Jamset, Jane Werry and Susan Wynne Roberts

**R. RHINEGOLD EDUCATION**

www.rhinegoldeducation.co.uk

## Music Study Guides

GCSE, AS and A2 Music Study Guides (AQA, Edexcel and OCR)
GCSE, AS and A2 Music Listening Tests (AQA, Edexcel and OCR)
AS/A2 Music Technology Study Guide (Edexcel)
AS/A2 Music Technology Listening Tests (Edexcel)
Revision Guides for GCSE (AQA, Edexcel and OCR), AS and A2 Music (Edexcel)

### Also available from Rhinegold Education

Key Stage 3 Listening Tests: Book 1 and Book 2
AS and A2 Music Harmony Workbooks
GCSE and AS Music Composition Workbooks
GCSE and AS Music Literacy Workbooks
Romanticism in Focus, Baroque Music in Focus, Film Music in Focus, Modernism in Focus,
*The Immaculate Collection* in Focus, *Who's Next* in Focus, *Batman* in Focus, *Goldfinger* in Focus, Musicals in Focus
Music Technology from Scratch
Dictionary of Music in Sound

First published 2013 in Great Britain by
Rhinegold Education
14–15 Berners Street
London W1T 3LJ, UK
www.rhinegoldeducation.co.uk

© 2013 Rhinegold Education
a division of Music Sales Limited

You should always check the current requirement of the examination, since these
may change. Copies of the OCR Specification can be downloaded from the OCR website at www.ocr.org.uk
or may be purchased from OCR Publications, PO Box 5050, Annesley, Nottingham NG15 0DL
Telephone: 0870 770 6622 Email: publications@ocr.org.uk

**OCR AS Music Study Guide 5th edition**
Order No. RHG208
ISBN 978-1-78305-222-6

Exclusive Distributors:
Music Sales Ltd
Distribution Centre, Newmarket Road
Bury St Edmunds, Suffolk IP33 3YB, UK
Printed in the EU

# Contents

(*) The first three jazz recordings in this list are set for examinations in June 2014 while the remaining three are set for examinations in June 2015 and June 2016.

The details of the specification are believed to be correct at the time of going to press, but you and your teachers should always check current requirements for the examination with OCR since these may change. The music specification is available at www.ocr.org.uk.

4

## The authors

**Huw Ellis-Williams** was brought up in Bangor and studied in Oxford and Exeter. A pianist, organist and part-time composer, he teaches at a comprehensive school in north Wales where he is head of sixth form. Huw has a particular interest in instrumental music of the early 20th century, and in music for theatre and film. He is an examiner for OCR. He has contributed to *Classroom Music* and is co-author of the Rhinegold *OCR A2 Music Study Guide*.

**Veronica Jamset** taught music in primary and secondary schools in both the state and private sectors in the West Midlands before taking up her first post in Higher Education as a teacher trainer. She worked in two colleges in Birmingham and then moved to St Mary's College at Strawberry Hill in Twickenham, where she became principal lecturer in music and director of in-service and continuing education. Veronica also has considerable experience in adult education. She has been an examiner at various levels since 1990 and, until 2000, was chief examiner for OCR's AS and A-level music syllabuses. She was a member of the team that drafted OCR's current AS/A2 music specification and continues to work as an examiner, reviser and syllabus developer.

**Jane Werry** read Music at Cambridge University, and has been Director of Music at Hayes School in Bromley since 1999. At Hayes she shares responsibility for professional development in teaching and learning. In 2013 her department was a finalist in the Best School Music Department category of the Music Teacher Awards for Excellence. Jane is an A level composition moderator for OCR, a member of TeachTalk:Music, and is also a frequent contributor to *Music Teacher* magazine. She is one of the authors of *Teaching Music: Practical Strategies for KS3* (Rhinegold Education, 2013). Alongside her education activities, Jane has always maintained a performing schedule, regularly singing around South East England in light opera, oratorio and pop. She is also an enthusiastic ukulele player, running and performing in various community bands.

**Susan Wynne Roberts** holds a Master's degree in Composing, Analysis and Criticism from the University of Surrey. She has taught music in a wide range of schools, and has been a principal examiner and moderator for composing at A level, both nationally and internationally, since 2000. She was a member of the team that wrote the current OCR specification and has developed well-received materials and resources for A-level teachers. Sue is an enthusiastic advocate of 20th-century and contemporary music; her interest in the way composers learn to compose has taken her as far afield as Boston and Athens. Sue continues to teach, as well as studying and working with the therapeutic aspects of music improvisation. A key focus of her interests is the mysterious and magical way in which music and memory work together.

# Introduction

## Course overview

There are three units in the AS music examination for OCR:

➤ Performing Music 1
  (worth 40% of the total AS mark)

➤ Composing 1
  (worth 30% of the total AS mark)

➤ Introduction to Historical Study in Music (sometimes called the 'listening paper', worth 30% of the total AS mark).

All units are now examined in the summer each year.

> OCR stands for 'Oxford, Cambridge and Royal Society of Arts'. It is the organisation that decides what you have to do in each part of this exam, supervises the marking, and awards grades and certificates.

### Performing

An examiner will come to your centre to hear your performance and discuss it with you. This will happen sometime during the second half of the spring term (March/April) or the beginning of the summer term – you will be told the precise date in advance.

### Composing

Your teacher will assess your composing throughout the course and send an overall mark to OCR with samples of your work (which you will probably choose together). This usually happens early in the summer term. OCR's moderator checks through the work to make sure that all the assessment criteria have been met and that standards are being maintained. If the moderator does not agree with your teacher's assessments (if they're too generous or too harsh) the mark can be changed (up or down). This ensures that your mark is in line with national standards.

### Introduction to Historical Study in Music

You will sit a two-hour written paper for which you will be given an individual copy of a CD to listen to on your personal stereo in the exam room. Some of the extracts will be from music that you are not expected to have heard before, but others will be from the set works you have studied. The questions will assume that you are *thoroughly familiar* with *all* of the set works. Make sure at the beginning of the course that you know exactly which six pieces you must study – they are listed on page 69.

AS Music is a qualification in its own right. Perhaps you are taking it because you enjoy music and want to broaden your course beyond the subjects that you are planning to take forward to A2. If you work steadily on all three units you will not find it a burden at the end of the course. Performing is usually out of the way by Easter, your composing portfolio will have been submitted at the very beginning of the summer term, and the written examination will not require a lot of last-minute cramming if you have got to know all the music early in your course.

AS is also the first stage of the complete A level in Music: if you intend to go on to A2 you will find that everything you have done at AS has provided you with a firm foundation for the next stage. The A2 units have similar titles and are examined in similar ways.

## How this guide will help you

Each unit has a separate chapter that tells you precisely what OCR expects you to do. We have set out all the content in detail and have given you advice on how to prepare.

Although the three units are assessed separately, a common thread runs through them all. This comes from two **areas of study**:

➤ **Tonality** is about a particular aspect of the language of music and will play an important part in your work for the first half of the composing unit

➤ **The Expressive Use of Instrumental Techniques** is about how to use instruments effectively, particularly in different combinations, and will be the focus of your work for the second half of the composing unit.

Many of the questions in the listening paper will focus on both of these areas of study. 'The Expressive Use of Instrumental Techniques' is also relevant to Performing Music 1, particularly if you intend to offer an ensemble or composition in Section C.

The chapters on each unit point out clearly how these two areas of study are involved but there is also a short chapter (starting on page 17) which explains them both. Don't be put off the first time you read this chapter if you don't see immediately how it applies to the music you know best. If you come back to it towards the end of your course you will find that you have learned to understand the chapter through *applying* the various points it contains.

### Exercises and practice questions

Throughout this book there are short exercises that have been designed to help you understand how what you have read applies to the music you are studying. At the end of each section on the set works there is a group of practice questions. These are not intended to be mini-exam papers but they will give you practice in answering the sorts of question that are often asked in the listening paper. Working through them will also help you to form ways of thinking that will stand you in good stead in the examination.

## How you can help yourself

Preparing for the performing unit obviously requires regular practice; exercises for the composing unit must be done throughout the course, not all in the last couple of weeks; and learning about the set works for the listening paper will need plenty of time for you to get to know all six pieces really well. So, you need to plan your time – what you will do each week – and draw up a timetable that shows how and when you will complete all the different parts of your work.

But your AS music course is not a set of unrelated hoops that you must keep jumping through. Although each bit has to be examined separately, all your musical activities support one another:

➤ Being a performer will help you to understand composing and listening

➤ Being a composer will help you to understand performing and listening

➤ Being a perceptive listener will help you to understand your own performing and composing better.

When you do any of these things you are being a *musician* and you will gradually discover, as you work through this book, that everything you learn about music is related:

➤ A detail of how a trumpeter plays in a jazz piece might set you thinking about how trumpets were played in much earlier music, or might give you an idea for your own composing or improvising

➤ Thinking about the structure of one of the pieces you are going to play in your recital will help you shape the music more convincingly and give you extra practice in analysing harmony and form

➤ Working out which notes are harmony notes in a melody for your Section A composing coursework will help you to phrase your own performances intelligently and will prepare you for Section A of the listening paper

➤ Listening to a range of music will help you show an awareness of style and conventions in your own performing.

Because the requirements for Section A of your composing coursework and Section B of the listening paper are fairly precise, we have been able to explain these in plenty of detail to help everyone. But *you* choose all the music you will perform and *you* decide what style of piece to compose for Section B of the composing unit. We can give you quite a lot of general guidance about these and your teachers will give you a great deal of help and encouragement, but the final decisions are yours.

The more you try to make connections for yourself between the different elements of your course, the wiser your decisions will be. If you aim to be a rounded musician who experiences music as a whole, the sooner all the separate elements will fall into place.

# Performing

An examiner will come to your school or college to listen to you and discuss your performance with you. The whole performing exam will usually take about 20 minutes.

## Section A: Recital (60 marks)

First, you perform a short programme of pieces in which you must be the *soloist*. If you play an instrument which is normally accompanied, like the clarinet, or if you are a singer, then you will need an accompanist. The choice of music is up to you, but two or three contrasting pieces should be enough to give you scope to demonstrate a range of skills and show that you understand different styles.

Your programme should not last more than eight minutes. You do not have to perform for that length of time but if your programme is very short it is unlikely that it will let you show yourself off to best advantage.

## Section B: Discussion (20 marks)

After you have played or sung, the examiner will discuss your performance with you. This will not take longer than about five minutes.

## Section C: Extended performing (40 marks)

In this part of the examination you have to perform *in a different way from Section A*. You must choose one of the following:

1.  Performing a short programme (no more than four minutes long) on a *different* instrument (or voice).

2.  Performing in an ensemble or duet. If you play a chordal instrument, such as the piano or guitar, you can choose to perform as an accompanist for this option. Again, a short programme of no more than four minutes in length, is required. Note that:

    ➤ If you had an accompanist in Section A, you cannot do so again for this section and claim that you are now a 'duet' – the examiner needs to hear what *else* you can do

    ➤ The examiner will need to be able to hear your own contribution to the ensemble, so activities such as singing in a choir or playing a part that is doubled by other instruments would not be suitable for this option.

3.  Performing your own composition(s) on the *same* instrument or voice that you presented in Section A. At least one other instrument or voice must be involved – you cannot perform an unaccompanied solo for this option. Again, your programme should be no longer than four minutes and it may consist of just one piece or, at most, two pieces. You must hand a fully-notated

score of your composition(s) to the examiner before you begin your performance.

4. Improvising. The examiner will give you a choice of starting points and you will be allowed ten minutes to prepare. You may use any instrument (or voice). The starting points (some examples of which are shown right) will include:

➢ Four pitches (without rhythm)

➢ A melodic opening (in treble, bass or C-clef) which can be transposed to suit your instrument or voice

➢ A short unpitched rhythm

➢ A chord pattern (for which you may have an accompanist)

➢ A simple poem with an optional melodic opening.

For Section A (and possibly C) you have the option of performing in front of an audience, or in private. The audience cannot stay in the room during the Section B discussion.

## Preparing for the examination

Perhaps you really enjoy performing in public or perhaps you prefer playing or singing informally with just a small group of friends. You might even be someone who prefers creating your own new music, as a composer. Perhaps you really don't like being in the spotlight and enjoy exploring music by performing it out of earshot of other people. As musicians we all have different interests, strengths and weaknesses: it helps if we are honest with ourselves and recognise what they are, then we can exploit our strengths and work steadily on the bits that don't come quite so naturally. It often turns out to have been worth doing after all.

Even the most experienced international performers have nerves. It is rare for anyone to feel after a concert that it was the 'best I've ever done' – there's nearly always something they think didn't quite come off. Professionals are in a competitive world and always strive to be better – better than they were last year, better than their rivals. If you are hoping to take up a career as a performer then you will have to learn to live with this competitive self-criticism – competing with yourself to improve, competing with others to get the job. Being on top of your technique and knowing the music thoroughly must become a way of life for you.

For many of us, though, exploring music through performing it, interpreting it for ourselves rather than only hearing how other people do it, is one of the most enjoyable parts of developing as a musician. It is a way of getting inside music that will help us understand it better and feed our creative imagination as composers. The more we do, the more we will want to do: if we've got a butterfly nature, impatient to sample everything, we flit from composer to composer, genre to genre; if we tend to stick to one thing then we may get more and more deeply interested in one particular composer or type of music. Most likely you are somewhere in between, always pleased when the opportunity to

Pitch:

Melody:

Rhythm:

Chords:

| F | Dm | Gm | C |
| $F^7$ | B♭ | $C^7$ | F |

Poem:

Music, when soft voices die,
Vibrates in the memory –
Odours, when sweet violets sicken,
Live within the sense they thicken.

Rose leaves, when the rose is dead,
Are heaped for the beloved's bed;
And so thy thoughts, when thou art gone,
Love itself shall slumber on.
*(Shelley)*

Optional opening:

Mu - sic

learn a new piece comes along, but with a good handful of old favourites that you enjoy coming back to. Be curious and adventurous in your study. But, when it comes to an examination, *play safe.*

The performing exam is not a series of hurdles set up to see how far round the course you can get before you fall over: it is designed flexibly, to suit everyone, so that not just different instruments or types of voice are catered for, but different interests in music, different personal temperaments and different circumstances as well. On this occasion *you* choose all the music.

## The recital

Choose music you feel comfortable with. Discuss it with your teachers and listen to their advice. If you take lessons with an independent teacher outside your school or college make sure they know what the performing requirements are for OCR AS Music – show them this guide.

Don't rely on a single long piece to give you sufficient scope to show a range of skills and understanding. You need at least one other piece of contrasting music. But *how* contrasting? The music you choose should preferably be typical of the repertoire for the instrument. For instance, if you are a pianist, an arrangement of Pachelbel's *Canon* (originally written for strings and keyboard) is not really typical of piano repertoire and will only give you a very limited opportunity to show your understanding of the instrument. It is usually better to play pieces that were designed with the instrument you are playing in mind.

If you are primarily a jazz performer, 'contrasting' does not mean that you have to perform a Baroque work – you can play entirely jazz pieces, but make sure your programme includes music that uses different techniques and is in different jazz styles.

How difficult? You don't need to torture yourself by playing for a full eight minutes at the most extreme limit of your technical abilities. Include something that shows the best that you can do but remember that 'difficulty' isn't only about pyrotechnics – it's also about expressiveness and understanding the music. Choose at least one piece that lets you show what the instrument can express – perhaps a range of tone colours or dynamics, or a very legato singing line. But don't overreach yourself: what goes well when you are relaxed and totally immersed in the music may throw up unexpected problems when you find yourself in an unfamiliar situation.

It is not a good idea to perform without an accompanist if the music was intended by the composer to be accompanied. As the soloist, you need to be able to show that you can coordinate your solo part with the accompaniment. It is your responsibility to make the arrangements for an accompanist. This should be settled well before the examination date so that you have sufficient time to practise together and become comfortable with one another. You need to hear how the accompaniment goes at an early stage of learning the piece, not in the last few days before the exam. You will feel more secure if you know the accompaniment well – it will help to make your performance much more convincing.

If possible, find out which room or hall the examination will be held in, and try to practise there at least a week in advance. If you are a pianist, you will need plenty of time to get used to the piano in the room. If you play or sing with an accompanist, give your accompanist the opportunity to practise with you using that piano, and sort out where you are going to stand or sit so that you have good eye contact between you. Whether you intend to have an audience on the day or not, try your programme out in front of a group of people – friends, relatives or even the public.

Do all this in good time beforehand so that if unexpected problems arise (you find there's a page-turn that you can't manage without the music falling off the stand, or the noise of the air-conditioning hums distractingly through the quiet bits of the music) something can be done about them.

You will need to have copies of all your music ready to be sent to the examiner at least a week before the recital. Photocopies may be used. They will be taken away by the examiner for reference.

> The examiner's copies of your music will be returned later (or destroyed, in the case of photocopies).

## Discussion

The examiner will be interested to find out what you thought about as you prepared each piece – how you made your expressive choices, why you decided to perform a particular passage one way rather than another and whether you think it worked as intended in the performance you've just given. It is not about how many notes you slipped up on, or which bits were too difficult for you – you are not being asked to confess to performing badly – but about aspects of the music that may be less obvious: if you got faster somewhere in the middle of a piece, was this because the composer had marked it accelerando or because you felt the music really needed to push on at that particular moment? If the dynamic markings range from *pp* to *ff*, do you think the contrasts were sufficiently effective? What made you put that particular ornament in this phrase? Why did you slur the last two bars that way?

We practise writing about music, learn technical terms, and develop new skills to identify and describe what we hear. But talking about our own performance is not something we are often encouraged to do. In our lessons the usual routine is probably: you play, your teacher listens and then does the talking. And, much of the time, because we respect our teacher's judgement, if they say 'no, play the phrase this way' and then they demonstrate for you to copy, we do it: have you ever asked 'why'? 'Why?' is what the examiner is going to want to discover from you.

How can you practise for this part of the examination? Start by listening more closely to your friends when they perform and by trying to articulate a more detailed response than you would usually – not just 'that was great', but 'I liked the beginning and the end very much but am not so sure about the middle'. This might lead to a discussion about the effect that their performance had and you could both try to tease out why the outside parts were exciting but that middle bit was boring or dull or just lost momentum. Then invite them for a return match to listen to you and discuss your performance. This isn't enough for the discussion in the exam, but it's a way to get started thinking about why performances are the way they are – not just because your teachers have said 'do it my way' – and how people sometimes hear what we perform quite differently from what we assumed.

In Section B of the listening paper you will be asked to compare two different performances of a passage from one of the set orchestral scores or be asked questions about the performing style and technique of one of the musicians in the set jazz recordings. Reflecting on your own performing intentions and how effectively they came over in performance is the other side of this coin: when performing, *you* are the interpreter.

## Extended performing

The decision about which of the four options you are going to do needs to be taken fairly early. There are a number of practical considerations. Discuss all of the options thoroughly with your teachers before deciding.

If you are thinking of doing option 1 (performing on a second instrument or voice) the choice about which instrument to offer for the Section A recital and which one to offer here can be a tricky one if you are equally strong on both of them. Bear in mind that there are only 40 marks for this part of the examination, while the Section A recital is worth 60 marks. It makes sense to offer your stronger instrument in Section A.

If you want to take option 2 (performing in an ensemble or duet, or as an accompanist), then other performers will be involved and you need to begin to make arrangements for rehearsals as early as possible. Choosing and obtaining suitable music (particularly if your ensemble is not a common combination of instruments) may take longer than you expect. It needs to be something that everyone involved can manage comfortably, but that also stretches you (remember that your part must not be doubled by anyone else).

You also need to give yourself plenty of time to try out your different role – for example, you may never have accompanied anyone before and your soloist's choice of music might challenge you more than you expected. This option puts you into a different relationship with other performers – this time you are not the 'star performer' and you may have to learn some negotiating skills. Be prepared for some setbacks: if you are working with other students, they will be under pressure too, and your examination may not be at the top of their agenda. Agree a manageable rehearsal schedule in good time and stick to it.

If you choose option 3 (performing your own composition), you will obviously need to start drafting ideas, and then refining and completing the actual composition well before the examination.

You may use any instrument, or singing, for option 4 (improvising): it doesn't have to be the instrument you used in your recital. You may have no difficulty deciding which of the starting points is likely to be best for you. If you are a singer, it is sensible to choose the poem; if you're a guitarist, the chords; a drummer, the rhythm.

If you play a melody or keyboard instrument, you have more choice. A saxophone player, for instance, might choose the pitches, the melodic opening, the rhythm, or even the chords. If you play a melody instrument such as the flute and choose the chords as a starting point, you can have an accompanist to play the chords. The accompanist is allowed to practise with you in the ten-minute preparation time but is not allowed to help you with your own improvisation. If you are a keyboard player and choose the chords option, you are not allowed to play with another performer.

## On the day

You will be told the date of the examination in advance. The examiner will contact your teacher, probably during February, to arrange a time that is convenient for everyone. It may be before the end of the spring term or early in the summer term. Your teacher will draw up a timetable for the day and ask you for details of your programme. It is your responsibility to make sure that your accompanist, if you need one, and any other performers needed for your Section C option, all know the date and time, and confirm that they will be available.

The day before the examination, make sure that everything is organised – copies of the music, music stands, amplifiers and an audience, if you want one. Practise carefully in a quiet frame of mind, and have a good sleep. On the day, keep calm – let yourself breathe. Think positively – the examiner is not the enemy or an alien species. He or she is a musician, probably a teacher and possibly a parent as well, who understands the stress you are under. Very occasionally it may be a surprise when you walk into the examination room to find that that there are two examiners. This is done to make sure that examiners are all marking to the same standard across the country. It doesn't put you under twice as much as pressure!

> The whole examination will be recorded – this is a safeguard for you.

The examiner will probably say something welcoming when you come into the room. Listen carefully to everything the examiner says but don't try to read too much into it. If you are asked to wait a few moments between pieces, don't assume that what you've just done was so terrible that a whole essay is being written about it. If you've chosen a programme that goes on too long and the examiner stops you, don't jump to the conclusion that he or she couldn't stand any more – they are probably being very careful to keep to the timetable so that the next student is not kept waiting.

However carefully you've prepared, though, the unexpected can always happen – the fire alarm goes, a string breaks, your accompanist is ill and someone else stands in at the last moment. None of these signals the end of the world. Examiners have these things happen to them in their own day-to-day work as musicians and they understand the extra stress it puts you under. Don't panic – deal with the problem and carry on.

# Assessment

Most of us are naturally self-critical about our performing. The desire to improve is healthy and makes us practise but, because we're trying to get it 'right', we sometimes get into a habit of paying more attention to what is 'wrong' than what is going well. The job of our teachers, especially, is to point out what needs attention and how to overcome problems: we may sometimes feel that we can never satisfy them. This can result in our reflections about how we performed focusing too much on the negative aspects, always remembering what went wrong, instead of what worked well.

The job of an examiner is different from that of a teacher. It is to notice everything that you *can* do. Right from the start the examiner will be listening in a positive way, giving marks for what you achieve, not taking them away because of things that didn't go well. Examiners work to marking criteria that specify the range of marks available for various levels of performance. As you will see below, it is not just getting all the notes right that matters, there are other aspects of your performance that the examiner will consider.

The full marking criteria for Performing, along with detailed descriptions of the mark bands, are printed in Appendix B of the OCR Specification.

## Recital

Each of the following four categories of assessment is worth 15 of the total 60 marks available for the recital.

**Knowledge and fluency (of pitch and rhythm)**

This is an assessment of how well you know the music, how securely you have it in your head. Although it's partly about getting all the notes right, it's more about whether you are confident about where the music is going. If your fingers slip through nerves and the examiner feels that you nevertheless knew what you should have played, the 'fluff' will probably be overlooked.

This also applies if part of your performance involves improvisation: in this case it's not so much about accuracy as whether your musical ideas are fluent and what you play has a sense of direction.

**Technical control**

You may have learned the music thoroughly and understand a lot about how it ought to go, but can you actually get through it without falling over in passages that are really too difficult for you? This would be an obvious sign that you are not in technical control of your instrument (in this respect the voice is an 'instrument', too).

Although you want to show the very best of what you can do, it is always a mistake to perform music that you are not quite on top of. It will make you extra edgy when you really want to be able to concentrate on all the other aspects that matter. But the examiner will be listening for more than just whether you can perform the correct notes: a wide range of technical skills can be rewarded, some of them quite subtle, like balance between melody and chords or contrasts of tone-colours, as well as more obvious aspects like intonation, pedalling, breathing, tonguing or diction. Try to choose music that allows you to show different technical and expressive skills. If you are a pianist, include something that shows you can use the sustaining pedal, but don't play a whole programme of over-pedalled pieces; if you're a singer, make sure that you show you can sustain a melodic line without help from the piano – don't choose a programme that consists entirely of songs in which the accompaniment doubles the vocal part.

For most of us, the first category of marks, Knowledge and fluency, will be about knowing what the composer wrote on the page – the notes and rhythms. The marks under the third category, Realisation of performance markings and/or performing conventions, are for showing in your performing that you understand other sorts of signs such as tempo and dynamic markings, articulation, ornaments and some of the aspects of music that are not written down – the conventions associated with different types of music. These might include, for instance, playing quavers in a swung style in jazz, or deliberately unevenly (*notes inégales*) in some types of Baroque music, or adopting a flexible approach to tempo (*rubato*) where appropriate in Romantic music. In other words, the examiner will be listening to hear whether you are performing the music in the way that the composer would have expected it to sound.

Do you actually listen to the sounds you are making or are you too busy worrying about what comes next? If your intonation is a bit off, is it because you're not really listening to yourself or because, technically, you can't play it any more accurately? If you came in too soon, was it due to not knowing the music well enough or was it because you weren't listening to the accompaniment? And do you understand the different styles needed for a Bach minuet and a Chopin waltz, or a Mozart aria and a Lloyd Webber song? This is where your *musicianship* really shows.

## Discussion

The better you understand the styles of your pieces and know what to consider when performing them, then the more detailed you can be in your answers and so more of the 20 available marks can be awarded. If you want to, you can illustrate particular points by playing or singing a phrase or passage that you are discussing, *provided that it is relevant*. For instance, you might want to show that you had thought about which notes in a phrase to slur and which ones to detach: it could be appropriate to demonstrate and then discuss the differences, in order to explain why you chose to perform it the way you did.

Key phrases in OCR's description of the sort of discussion that would be worth between 13 and 16 of the 20 marks are: 'informed answers', 'clear awareness of expressive choices ... and of their effectiveness in performance'.

Although you will have no idea beforehand what questions about your performance the examiner will ask, you can be sure that there will be no trick questions designed to catch you out. The examiner will be keen to find what you *can* talk about – your communication skills are not being assessed and you will not lose marks just because you stumble over a word. And you have every reason to feel confident because *you* have chosen the music. You are not going to be asked about unfamiliar music. Provided you have thought about what you are doing, and why, as you prepared, and haven't been performing parrot-fashion or on autopilot, you should feel that you are on home territory.

## Extended performing

The marking criteria for the various extended performing options are mostly similar to those for the recital.

**Second instrument or voice**

The criteria for this option are identical to those for the recital, except that each of the four categories is marked out of ten rather than 15 marks.

**Duet, ensemble or accompanying**

This option requires extra aural and stylistic awareness – listening to the other performer(s), coordinating, knowing when to come to the fore and when to blend. In an improvisatory style (like a jazz group) the ability to extend musical ideas in a way that is appropriate to the style also comes into the picture. If a group uses amplifiers, the way they are managed to balance the performance may also be taken into account.

**Your own composition(s)**

This option is assessed in a similar way to Section B of the composing unit. There are ten marks for the score and the accuracy of its relationship to what is performed; ten marks for the way the composition shows your understanding of the technical and expressive possibilities of your instrument (or voice); a further ten marks for similar understanding of the other instruments or voices involved in the composition; and ten marks for the way the composition shows your aural awareness and understanding of the relationship between all the performers in the ensemble.

Notice that many of the marks in this option are awarded for composing skills. If composition is your strength, this is the place in the course where you could capitalise on it.

**Improvising**

For your improvisation there are ten marks available for fluency and form, ten for technical control, ten for imaginative use of the 'stimulus' (the starting point), and ten for your aural and stylistic awareness.

# The areas of study

Two areas of study have important roles in underpinning large sections of your AS course – ideas, techniques and various bits of information that relate to them will keep cropping up. You will find it helpful to keep them in mind in almost everything you do. Get your ears tuned in to recognising their relevance in whatever you are performing, composing or listening to.

## Tonality (The Language of Western Tonal Harmony)

Don't confuse tonality with 'tone colour', which means something completely different. Music that is **tonal** is music that uses one or more keys (as in major or minor).

The word **tonic** refers to the main key of a piece of music and its key chord (chord I). A piece of tonal music usually begins and ends in its tonic key and will probably pass through other keys (**modulate**) in between. These other keys are described as **related** if they contain many notes in common with the tonic – for example, the relative minor shares the same key signature as its relative major key – otherwise they are said to be **non-related**. Relationships between keys play an important structural role in a great deal of the music that you will hear and perform.

If the pitches in tonal music all come from the current key, the music is said to be **diatonic**. Pitches outside the current key that are used to add colour rather than to introduce a modulation, are called **chromatic** notes (chromatic means 'coloured').

The major and minor scales of the tonal system are not the only scales used in music. For example, until about 1600 various **modes** were used in European music. Some folk songs are modal, and a number of 19th- and 20th-century composers have used modes in their music to give it a folk or national flavour. Major and minor scales are sometimes thought of as two modes that survived after 1600.

By the end of the 19th century, tonal harmony had become so complex that a clear sense of related keys became increasingly obscured by the use of many chromatic notes. In the 20th century some composers experimented with non-tonal types of scale as a basis for organising their compositions. Today, some music is tonal and some is non-tonal. In your own work for Section B of the composing unit (and for the composing option in Section C of the performing unit) you are free to choose tonal or non-tonal styles, but your exercises for Composing Section A must be tonal.

The rejection of tonality by some composers after 1900 is sometimes described as the 'breakdown of tonality'. Of course, it did not actually die out. Many composers have continued to write in a broadly tonal style, and much western popular music (and even jazz) is essentially tonal in nature.

The word 'western' reminds us that it is mainly in the history of European (and later, American) music that tonality has had such a dominant role. Other civilisations (such as India and Japan) have used different systems. In Indian music, a *raga* sets out the melodic ingredients from which an improvisation will grow. As it progresses the audience recognises and appreciates the performer's uniquely personal expressive use of characteristic features of the *raga*.

In a similar way, although most of us are unaware of it as we listen to western tonal repertoire, we orientate ourselves at the beginning of a piece by fixing the tonic in our ears as 'the place we are starting from', and then recognise and enjoy the way the music travels away from it and comes home again at the end – a satisfying resolution to the story.

In a loose way we often use the metaphor of a language to describe the way tonality works. The parts of this language that you need to learn to handle confidently – the chords, cadences, modulations, passing notes and so on – are a little bit like parts of speech (nouns, verbs, conjunctions). This may be a useful way to think about the techniques and conventions but it doesn't mean that 16 bars of music will have a meaning in the way that a sentence does.

The specific features of western tonal harmony that you must learn to recognise and be able to handle are:

> Major and minor keys

> Diatonic intervals (major or minor 3rds and 6ths etc)

> Chords I to VII and their inversions; chords with an added 7th

> Perfect, imperfect, plagal and interrupted cadences, and other common chord progressions

> Modulation to closely-related keys (dominant, subdominant and the relative minor or relative major)

> Tonal devices such as sequence and pedal.

Above all you need to learn to recognise the harmonic implications of a melody or bass, and to develop a feel for how often the harmonies change (known as the **rate of harmonic change** or **harmonic rhythm**).

All the work you do in Section A of the composing unit is based on this area of study, and it also plays a large part in Sections A and B of the listening paper. Much of the music that you perform will also be in tonal styles, whether from the 17th, 18th, 19th, 20th or 21st centuries: understanding its tonal language will help you find suitable ways to shape such pieces expressively.

As we study the music of the 18th century we will become aware of various conventions – things that were common practice, although never 'rules'. For example, it was common for a piece to begin by making the tonic clear to the listener, perhaps by basing the melody on parts of a broken chord. But it was inevitable that one day somebody would have the idea of starting in a different, more ambiguous way.

In the exam, chord names may be given as well as Roman numerals (e.g. VI/Gm).

# The Expressive Use of Instrumental Techniques

If you took GCSE Music you will have learned something about individual instruments and the sounds that they are able to make, and you will already know quite a lot about the one you play yourself. In this area of study you learn more about performing techniques and how musicians use them for expressive effects. You will also learn about ways of *combining* instruments to produce different textures and sonorities.

Although this area of study is about instruments, if you are a singer it's worth thinking about vocal techniques in a similar way.

As a starting point, see what more you can discover about your own instrument: it may be able to do a great deal more than you are capable of producing on it at the moment. Listen to well-known performers. When you are sure you know your instrument inside out, compare it with similar instruments in terms of its range, registers (the different parts of the range), timbres (tone colours), agility and expressive power.

Your study of three orchestral scores and three jazz recordings for the listening paper will focus a great deal on techniques of performing and on ways of combining instruments. When you come to compose your own music for instrumental ensemble in Section B of the composing unit, the sounds you have been listening to, and the understanding you have gained about how these are produced, will provide you with a stock of techniques that you can draw on. You won't want to compose an 18th-century symphony or a 1920s' jazz standard – your own musical language will be different – but the textures and timbres you have studied may well be ones that linger in your imagination.

These pieces also provide the focus for your historical study: many instruments in the 18th century looked and sounded very different from the way they do now. You need to know about this. But there is also a great difference in the way composers scored for them at the beginning of the 18th century (Handel) and a hundred years later (Beethoven). Even during Mozart's lifetime the instruments themselves were changing. Jazz hasn't stood still, either: you will discover differences between the sounds that performers made in the 1920s and only 30 years later, even on the same type of instrument.

In your own performing, too, particularly if you are playing in an ensemble or singing in a choir, get into the habit of noticing who is doing what – playing or singing in unison, 3rds, imitation, contributing to widely- or tightly-spaced chords, throwing a motif from part to part in dialogue, presenting the melody in the lowest part and so on. Notice details of articulation, dynamics, phrasing and balance.

# Composing

Can composing be taught or learned in a conventional way? Without doubt, the more you know and understand about music – the more music of different composers, styles and genres you listen to – the more enthused, excited and equipped you will be as you venture into the creative world of composing.

Composing (as an AS level unit) sits between the Performing and Introduction to Historical Topics Units. Both of these teach us a lot about composing, and the approaches to improving in these units apply equally to composition. Becoming a skilled and successful performer takes regular practice – technical studies as well as the performance of the staple musical repertoire for your instrument. You will also learn from listening to performances and recordings of established champions of your chosen instrument(s). As a performer you are re-creating the creation of the composer. Your study of orchestral scores and jazz listening will help you understand how the composers have assembled their ideas in a larger framework and this, together with other skilled listening of music of your own choice, will act as a springboard for your own ideas.

Aim to practise your skills of composing regularly and be ready to modify, re-think, transform and extend your ideas. You are making choices all the time in composing. Think about your options remembering that your skills of discrimination, invention and intuition are constantly developing as you engage with all areas of music study.

Harmony is one of the key elements of music composition. The triad is central to western tonal harmony. You may already have learned something about chords and keys, either from GCSE Music or in studying for a music theory exam. It is also possible to learn a great deal about tonal harmony by being inquisitive and curious about the music you play and listen to. The music itself becomes your textbook.

The two sections in this coursework unit carry equal marks. Your final portfolio will contain:

> **Section A: The Language of Western Tonal Harmony** (45 marks)

Seven exercises, including one completed without help, under timed conditions.

> **Section B: Instrumental Techniques** (45 marks)

A composition or arrangement for between four and ten instruments with a maximum length of three minutes.

Your teacher, who is responsible for monitoring your work throughout the course, will mark your composition portfolio. Samples of work from your centre will be sent to OCR to ensure that the assessment is fair and meets the required standards.

At first glance, the two sections of this unit may appear to be quite separate in their demands. The work in Section A will enable you to become familiar with the practices and conventions of tonality (a system that has been the backbone of western music for several centuries). Section B allows for a more personal extension of your composing ideas. Many of the basic concepts studied in Section A will be relevant to your work for Section B, whatever choices of language, style or genre you make. Both involve studying music by established composers to use as models of best composing practice.

# Section A: Western Tonal Harmony

To begin with, your teacher may introduce you to the basics through shorter exercises. These exercises may include 'sign-posts' to help you with harmonic or textural decisions. As you become more confident you should be able to work independently without hints or prompts.

Your exercises will consist of a complete melody plus the opening notes of the complete texture. This is sometimes referred to as the 'incipit'. The melodies used must be by established composers. You will consider the harmonies suggested by the music, derive a suitable bass part and write in chord symbols to show your understanding of the choices you make. In at least two exercises you will need to show the harmonies in full with a complete texture based on the model of the given opening.

An explanation of the timed exercise, along with advice on the selection of your final six exercises, is given on pages 41–42.

It is essential to hear the music you are working with in this unit. The exercises in this study guide will help ensure that the concepts described come to life in a practical way for you. Your teacher will often play examples to you. You may also want to consult any of the harmony textbooks listed for extra preliminary exercises and further help.

*AS Music Harmony Workbook* by Hugh Benham. Rhinegold, 2008, ISBN 978-1-906178-34-5.

*Harmony in Practice* by Anna Butterworth. ABRSM Publishing, 1999, ISBN 978-1-854728-33-3.

*The ABC of Harmony* series by Roy Wilkinson. Boosey and Hawkes.

*The Dynamics of Harmony: Principles and Practice* by George Pratt. Oxford University Press, 1984/1996, ISBN 978-0-198790-20-4.

*Harmony* by Walter Piston. W. W. Norton & Co. Ltd, 1988, ISBN 978-0-393-95480-7.

## Getting started

You will need a working understanding of staff notation in both treble and bass clefs. If your reading skills are not very fluent do not worry: with practice you will improve and the rewards are well worth the effort. In addition you will need to know about:

➢ Keys, intervals, scales

➢ Chords and cadences.

Remember that working with chords, bass lines and melodies is a musical activity: try not to view it as 'theory'. Take every opportunity to observe what is happening in the music by using your ears and eyes as well as developing your understanding.

In questions for your historical unit, you will need to identify keys, modulations and individual chords, and be able to analyse sections of the harmonic structure.

## Understanding chords

A method of labelling the degrees of the scale on which the triads are formed was developed in the early 19th century; this method uses Roman numerals beneath the stave. This chapter will use: upper case numerals for major chords; lower case for minor; italics for other types of chord.

A checklist is provided on page 42 to help you make sure that your portfolio includes a suitable range of skills and understanding.

The diatonic triads are made up of 3rds superimposed on each degree of the scale. These are described as 'root position' chords.

You will notice that two of the chords, ii and V, have a further third superimposed above the triad: counting from the root note, it is a 7th above. Chords with an added 7th are a common feature of the harmonic language of western music.

### Chord voicing and labels

The triads in the previous example are in **close position**; their notes are as close together as possible. Play them through slowly on a keyboard instrument; first without the added 7th on ii and V, and then with it included. Can you hear that some of the triads sound major and some minor? The triad on the leading note is a diminished triad and sounds rather different.

close position          open position

The harmony will sound more effective if the notes of the chord are more widely spaced in what is called open position. The way the notes are distributed in a chord is called the voicing. There are many possibilities when using open position chords; some different voicings of a C major chord are shown left.

So long as the degree of the scale on which the triad is built remains at the bottom of the chord, the chord is said to be in root position – no matter how many notes there are above or how they are arranged. When a different note of the chord is in the bass, the chord is known as an inverted chord. If the:

➤ 3rd of the chord is in the bass (the lowest note), the chord is in **first inversion**

➤ 5th of the chord is in the bass (the lowest note), the chord is in **second inversion**

➤ 7th of the chord is in the bass (the lowest note), the chord is in **third inversion.**

Notice in the following example (in D major) how each chord inversion is indicated by adding 'b', 'c' or 'd' to the Roman numeral that describes the chord:

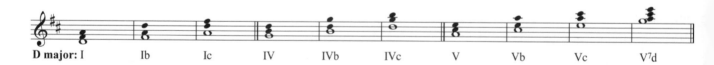

Chords in root position, and in first or third inversion, are freely used when harmonising melodies; second inversions are used less freely and in the special circumstances described on page 34.

If you are a guitarist or jazz pianist you may be familiar with a different style of chord labelling, positioned above the stave. This system of notation uses the letter name of the root of the chord. If a letter name appears by itself it is assumed to be major. If the triad is minor, the letter name is followed by 'm' or 'min', while 'dim' after the letter indicates a diminished triad. Inversions are shown by writing the chord name followed by an oblique symbol – or forward slash '/' – and then the name of the bass note. For example, C/E is a first inversion chord of C major, with E as the

Why are there two methods for labelling chords? Roman numerals show the function of the chord in relationship to the given key: for example, a chord V is always the dominant chord whatever key the music is in at that point. Letter names show immediately what notes are to be played regardless of the overall key: if the chord is C, you play C, E, and G.

lowest note in the bass. In some of the examples that follow both
systems are used.

1. On a keyboard instrument – right hand only – play some triads in their various root and inverted
   positions in as many keys as you can. Play through the example below to begin with, and then move
   to some other keys.

2. Play and label each of the triads in the examples below. Use either Roman numerals or chord symbols,
   and show the type of inversion when the chord is not in root position. The first answer is given.

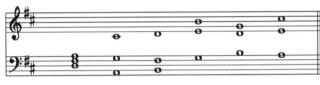

## Harmonising melodies

There is a great deal of flexibility in the choice and type of melodies
that can be worked for the Section A exercises. This allows you to
start from your own experience and performing abilities. You should
also aim to cover new ground as you explore the range of music
that uses western tonal harmony. Some examples of suitable
material might include:

➢ Traditional folk songs

➢ Simple popular songs from the 19th and early 20th centuries

➢ 18th-century keyboard pieces

➢ Hymn settings

➢ Early classical string quartets

➢ Short, simple pieces from the Romantic period.

You may begin by working with well-known melodies. For later
exercises, however, it is best to avoid tunes that you are aurally very
familiar with because these do not allow you to make judgements
about the choice of harmony for yourself.

**Melodies in a major key**   The melody of a piece contains many clues about the harmony and bass line possibilities. When harmonising a melody for the first time, familiarity with the melody is a very important starting point: play or sing it through several times.

*Amazing Grace*

Using the example above, aim to get a sense of the phrase lengths and where the cadence points lie at the end of each phrase. A phrase is often likened to a sentence. As in this example, it is useful to mark the ends of phrases with a tick (the place where a singer would take a breath) and / or draw a phrase mark in the appropriate place on the score.

## Exercise 2

1. Copy out the notes of the melody for *Amazing Grace*, from the example above.

2. Notice how each of the four phrases begins with an **anacrusis** (upbeat) of one crotchet beat before the bar line. Draw in the phrase marks and indicate the end of each phrase with a tick.

3. Your ear will often guide you as you think about where the harmony should change. Sing or play the melody with an accompaniment of a single tonic chord of G throughout (strummed guitar or piano vamp); it should feel 'uncomfortable' at those places in the melody where the harmony needs to be changed.

**Selecting chords in a major key**   The melody for *Amazing Grace* is in the key of G major. The example below shows the range of (diatonic) chords available in G major to harmonise this melody.

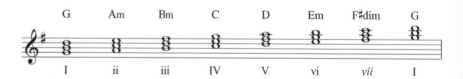

At this point, your first question is: 'Which chords should I use?' In both major and minor keys, chords I, IV and V are known as the **primary triads**, as they are the most commonly used chords in harmony. The most important triad of all is I, the tonic chord, which shares the letter name of the key. Many pieces start and finish on the tonic chord. The second most important chord is V, the dominant chord. The most commonly used **secondary triads** are ii and vi, although chord iii is also occasionally used. In a major key, chords I, IV and V are **major** triads, and chords ii, iii and vi are **minor** triads.

The earlier section on 'Understanding chords' in this chapter (page 21) introduced briefly the concept of **7th chords**. Adding the 7th above the root of a triad results in a four-note chord. The two most common 7th chords are those on the dominant ($V^7$) and the supertonic ($ii^7$). The **dominant 7th** is often used instead of a plain dominant triad in a perfect cadence, $V^7$–I; it is one of the strongest ways to confirm the tonality of a piece of music. Chord $ii^7$ often precedes $V^7$ at a cadential point: $ii^7$–$V^{(7)}$–I.

Understanding the function of primary and secondary triads within a key opens up a basic framework to harmonise a melody. Therefore, you now have the following chords to draw from for your harmonisation of *Amazing Grace* in the key of G major:

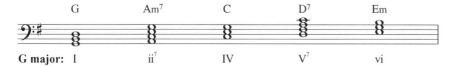

**Cadences**

We have already noted that cadences 'punctuate' the phrases of a melody, just as punctuation separates clauses and sentences in English grammar. The two most commonly used are:

➢ The **perfect cadence** consists of the progression V–I at the end of a phrase and brings a temporary or permanent halt to the music (like a 'full stop')

➢ The **imperfect cadence** uses any chord (I, ii, iib, and IV are the most frequent possibilities) followed by chord V at the end of a phrase. This cadence has an inconclusive effect rather like a comma; the music has more to say.

Two other cadences occurring less frequently are:

➢ The **plagal cadence** has a conclusive effect and consists of the chords IV–I. It is sometimes likened to the sound of a sung 'Amen' in sacred choral music

➢ The **interrupted cadence** is most usually represented by the progression V–vi. The harmonic flow (or pull) towards the tonic has been 'interrupted'. This cadence is often used to build tension in a piece of music. It increases the sense of anticipation before the stronger perfect cadence follows, confirming the tonic key.

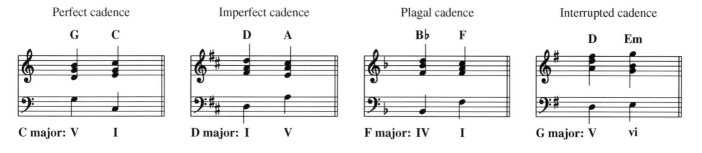

## Exercise 3

In the opening section (up to bar 23) of the Allegro in Handel's Trumpet Minuet HWV 349/13, identify each of the perfect and imperfect cadences. Note their 'finished' or 'unfinished' quality.

**Melodies in a minor key**    Below is an example of a traditional English melody in a minor key. Included in this example is an 'incipit' – a starting point that provides plucked guitar chords for you to continue in a similar style. To harmonise this melody, approach it in the same way as covered in the preceding section on major keys. Namely, sing or play the melody to become familiar with it; identify the key; mark in the phrases and the cadence points; and then identify the diatonic primary and secondary triads that could be used to harmonise the melody. (As you become familiar with the melody, you may recognise with your ears that there is a key change after the repeat of the first phrase at bar 5.)

Traditional English: *The Miller of Dee*

**Relative keys**    At first glance you might think that *The Miller of Dee*, with a key signature of a single flat, is in the key of F major. However, remember that every key signature has two possibilities: a major key and a relative minor key. The tonic of the relative minor is three semitones lower than the tonic of the major key. The D in bars 1 and 12, together with the raised 7th (C♯), confirm that *The Miller of Dee* is in D minor rather than F major.

**Minor scales**    There are two main types of minor scale: **harmonic minor** and **melodic minor**. The following three examples use a key signature of a single flat to illustrate the relationship between the relative keys.

F major

D harmonic minor

D melodic minor

As the name suggests, the harmonic minor scale is the one used primarily for writing harmony in the minor key. Notice that the 7th degree (leading note) is raised by a semitone, and that the ascending and descending versions of the melodic minor scale are slightly different. On the way up, both the 6th and the 7th degrees are raised by a semitone. However, on the way down both notes are restored to their 'natural' pitches (in other words, using only the pitches of the relative major key). As its name suggests, the melodic minor is preferred for melody writing because it avoids the awkward sound of the interval of the augmented 2nd between the 6th and 7th notes of the harmonic minor scale. (In D harmonic minor, the augmented 2nd is B♭ to C♯.)

## Exercise 4

Scales and arpeggios can be the raw materials for ideas and patterns that feature strongly in classical scores.

1. The following extract is found in Beethoven's Symphony No. 5, Allegro.

> ➤ Write out the C minor scale in both the *harmonic* and *melodic* versions.

> ➤ In the extract above circle the third quaver from bar 4 onwards to understand how this pattern is built from the descending scale.

> ➤ Where does the pattern change?

2. Choose an additional minor scale that you can play on your own instrument. Play the related major scale as well as the two versions of the minor scale (one octave for each scale, ascending and descending) until you are really familiar with the difference in sound between them. Devise your own exercises using the type of scalic patterns you have observed in Beethoven's score.

**Selecting chords in a minor key**

The function of chords is to support and complement the melody. Therefore, each minor chord has to be adaptable so that it can fit with melody notes from either the melodic or the harmonic minor scale. The stave below shows some of the most frequent versions of chords that can be used in the minor keys, using D minor as an example. (Chord VI, a major chord in a minor key, can often be used with stunning effect.)

Your portfolio should include at least one exercise in a minor key. The melody should be clearly minor – avoid folk tunes such as *Scarborough Fair* and *Greensleeves* that are modal rather than minor.

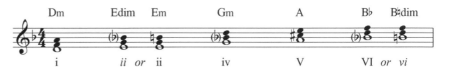

If you need to use a diminished triad, a good tip is to remember that it works best in first inversion with a doubled 3rd – the same applies to chord vii in major and minor keys.

**Harmonic rhythm**

The rate at which the harmony changes in relation to the melody is called the **harmonic rhythm**. In hymns and chorales (German hymn tunes) chords usually change on almost every beat of the bar. But in other types of melody the harmony usually changes less frequently – perhaps one or two chords per bar (for example, the opening bars of Mozart's horn concerto). In some cases the same chord may extend over three or more bars of music (for example, Beethoven's 5th Symphony movement 1, bar 44 onwards.

Up to half of the exercises in your portfolio can be harmonisations of hymn or chorale melodies, if you wish. But the remainder should show different rates of harmonic rhythm where you have to think carefully about the best places to make chord changes.

Sometimes the rate of harmonic change will increase at important cadences. If you look at the Welsh melody below, *The Ash Grove*, you will notice that only one chord per bar is needed for most of the tune (and a tonic chord could be used for the whole of bars 1–2). However, two different chords are needed in bar 7 to prepare for the perfect cadence in the final two bars.

Welsh Air: *The Ash Grove*

## Exercise 5

1. Harmonise the following melody by writing a suitable chord in each box, either above or below the stave using the appropriate symbols. Think carefully about which chord would work best before the perfect cadence at the end of the phrase.

*Amazing Grace*

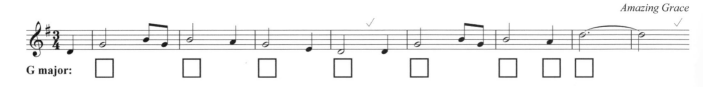

2. Choose suitable chords for the following melody by writing appropriate symbols in the correct positions either above or below the stave. The first two bars have been completed for you – notice that each chord lasts for two crotchet beats, and that a chord is placed on the rest at the start of bar 2. There is no need to increase the harmonic rhythm at the final cadence for this melody.

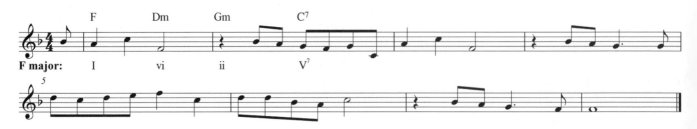

Melodies can give harmonic 'clues' by including broken-chord patterns as part of their structure.

## Non-harmony melody notes

J. S. Bach: Minuet in G

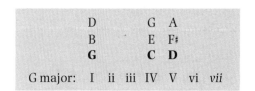

This example is in G major, the primary triads of which are shown right for reference. The melody implies harmony very clearly. The first four notes in bar 1 belong to chord I, while the next two could be harmonised with chord V (requiring D in the bass). The tonic is emphasised in bar 2, so a return to chord I would be better here than using chord IV (which also contains the tonic). Bars 3–4 are a repeat of the first two bars. In bar 5 there are only two notes, E and G. If we add C as a bass note, we have all the notes of chord IV. Which chord is suggested by bar 6?

Melodies based entirely on harmony notes can result in rather angular contours caused by the many **leaps** involved. Most tunes create a smoother outline by including **stepwise movement**:

Petzold / J. S. Bach: Minuet in G

The five notes in bar 1 are not contained in any one chord, so it is necessary to deduce which notes are harmony notes and which are not. We know that many tonal pieces begin with the tonic chord, which in G major has the notes G–B–D. In bar 1 of the Minuet example, the notes D, G and B fall on the first, second and third beats of the bar, respectively. Therefore, chord I is the obvious choice for bar 1.

The notes printed in grey (in bars 1 and 3) are not part of the chord for that bar; they are known as 'non-harmony notes'.

The non-harmony notes in the Petzold/Bach minuet example are known as **passing notes** because they pass by stepwise movement between the notes of the chord. Passing notes always move by step. They never leap to or from harmony notes, and they usually occur in rhythmically weak positions (here on quavers, after beats 2 and 3). As a result the passing dissonances they create are hardly noticeable.

You may find that 'non-harmony notes' are referred to elsewhere as 'inessential notes' or 'embellishing notes'.

Sometimes passing notes do fall on the beat, in which case they are described as **accented passing notes**. Such notes also move by step between harmony notes. However, because accented passing notes occur on the beat, the dissonance they produce against the underlying chord is more noticeable and often very expressive. The example in the right margin shows the accented passing notes circled. When the dissonant note moves by step to a harmony note we say it has **resolved**.

Mozart: Rondo, K. 485

G major:  I_____

Auxiliaries:

**Auxiliary notes** decorate or embellish the harmony notes by moving to the note above (an upper auxiliary) or below (a lower auxiliary) and then back again.

In the example given in the left margin, the auxiliary notes fall rhythmically on the weak parts of the beat. If the non-harmony notes have accidentals, we refer to them as **chromatic auxiliary notes**. In the example that follows, from Beethoven's Symphony No. 5 (first movement, bars 101-110), the phrase opens with lower chromatic auxiliary notes on the weak parts of the beat.

Beethoven: Symphony No. 5, *Allegro con brio*

Appoggiatura:

Suspension:

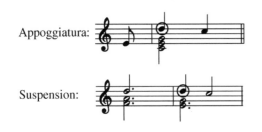

Another type of non-harmony note is the **appoggiatura**. The appoggiatura is similar to the accented passing note, except that it is approached by a leap rather than by step.

A similar non-harmony note, which creates a delay in the sounding of all the pitches of a chord together, is the **suspension**. A suspension occurs when a harmony note from a previous chord is held on or repeated while a new chord is sounded beneath it (rather than jumping to the dissonance, as in the appoggiatura). The prolonged note is described as a 'preparation'. When the chord beneath it changes, the held note becomes the 'suspension', which creates a dissonance with the new underlying harmony. The dissonant note then moves by step to a note of the new chord, which creates a 'resolution'.

To help remember the difference between an appoggiatura and a suspension, remember that a suspension must always include 'preparation, suspension, resolution'; whereas an appoggiatura has no preparation note and does not have to be approached by step.

From the second bar of the extract, circle the harmony and non-harmony notes, identifying notes that are suspensions, and the use of the appoggiatura in the violin part.

**Exercise 6**

The first phrase of the traditional melody below has a flowing accompaniment pattern.

1.  Within the melody, identify the: harmony notes; passing notes; and a preparation note for a suspension that follows.

Traditional: *Flow Gently Sweet Afton*

2.  Add in the correct chord symbols beneath the bass stave.

3.  Using your ear (and/or an instrument to help), notate a simple melody and harmonise it using appropriate chord symbols: for example, the first eight bars of *Skip to My Lou*. Once you have it sketched out, decorate the melody by including the following embellishments: passing notes and upper/lower (chromatic) auxiliaries. Can you use a suspension in the harmonic accompaniment?

## Writing a bass part

With your key, melody and chords decided, the next element to consider when harmonising a melody is writing a bass part. A simple bass line can be derived from the root notes of each harmonising triad. A much more interesting and 'melodic' bass line can be shaped by using chord inversions and non-harmony notes to create a smoother part.

The two examples that follow both show the first four bars of *Twinkle Twinkle Little Star*. The bass line for the first example comprises the root notes of each of the chosen chords. In the second example, the bass line uses root notes, first inversions, passing notes, and also adds more harmonic movement in preparation for the cadence. As a result, the second version offers stylistic character and a smoother, more lyrical shape. See if you can describe the function of each note of the bass line in the second version as either a harmony note, passing note, or auxiliary note. (You could also try inventing an alternative bass line of your own.)

*Twinkle Twinkle Litte Star*

*Twinkle Twinkle Litte Star*

The example below shows the first eight bars of Minuet in G. As with the second version of *Twinkle Twinkle Little Star*, the melody for Minuet in G is supported by a well-shaped bass part that makes use of first-inversion chords and passing notes. However, you will notice that there is less movement in the bass line in Minuet in G, to help balance the faster quaver movement in the melody. In addition, note how the bass in bar 8 retains the quaver momentum at a point where the melody itself lacks rhythmic interest.

Petzold / J. S. Bach: Minuet in G

## Exercise 7

This exercise will help you to gain practical experience of the sound and shape of well-constructed bass lines.

1. Choose an extract from *either* a classic popular song (such as Ben E. King's *Stand By Me* or *Penny Lane* by the Beatles) or a movement from a Baroque instrumental piece (a woodwind sonata, for example).

   ➤ Copy out the melody and bass part as accurately as possible (by hand or using notation software). Assign two appropriate instruments of your choice, for example, violin and cello or flute and bass guitar. Remember to think carefully about the issues involved if you choose to use a transposing instrument.

   ➤ Perform the piece, and listen to the strength of the two outer parts.

2. Working with a friend, play through some of the keyboard pieces in the *Notebook for Anna Magdalena Bach* by J. S. Bach. Take one hand each: one of you performing the melody; the other on the bass line. Many of these pieces are written for two parts only: Nos 4, 6, 7 and 18 are all good choices.

3. Sing or play through the soprano and bass parts only from some traditional hymn settings.

4. Play the violin and cello parts from extracts of Baroque instrumental works. Start with the Menuet, Lentement and Bourrée from Handel's *Water Music* Suite No. 2 in D.

In all of these exercises, notice how the bass parts are like melodies in their own right. Even though they generally have a larger number of wide leaps, they still create interesting lyrical shapes. It is possible to play many simple pieces with just the two outer parts (melody and bass); your 'inner ear' will fill in the harmonies even if they are not played.

# Chord progressions

Certain ways of assembling chords in a sequence or progression found widespread acceptance over a period of music history and established the language of Western tonal harmony we are so familiar with today.

In general it is useful to think about:

 ➢ Chord progressions that lead up to a cadence point

 ➢ Commonly found sequences of chords between the start and end of phrases.

The two most important notes in a scale are the tonic and dominant notes; they are related to each other by the interval of a perfect 5th. Chords that relate to each other because their roots are a 5th apart form very strong chord progressions. This is why various combinations of chords ii, V and I work so well at cadences.

Here are some chord progressions that are frequently used to establish a perfect cadence:

1.  In the first progression, the roots of the chords can be clearly seen, each spaced a 5th apart.

2.  The root of chord ii in the lower octave gives the bass line a better shape. This demonstrates an important principle very well: that a rising 4th is effectively the same as a falling 5th.

3.  By using the first inversion of chord ii the bass line achieves a smoother shape.

4.  A common variation of the ii–V–I chord progression uses a second inversion of chord I immediately before the final two chords of a perfect cadence. (This progression is also described as a 'cadential 6-4'.)

Second inversion chords are also known as $^6_4$ chords because the upper notes are a 6th and 4th above the bass part. This method of indicating harmony, called **figured bass**, was used in the Baroque period.

We can apply the principle that strong progressions have roots that fall in 5ths to longer chord sequences. If the roots of a chord progression keep moving down in perfect 5ths or up in perfect 4ths, a pattern known as a complete circle of 5ths is produced. Notice how all 12 notes of the chromatic scale are sounded before the circle returns to the starting pitch.

## Circle of 5ths

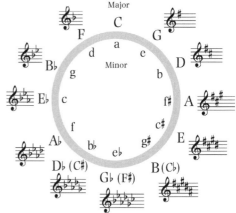

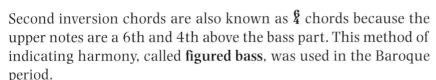

Notice how all 12 notes of the chromatic scale are sounded before the circle returns to the starting pitch (in this example, to the C an octave lower). To simplify the notation, the example changes from flats to sharps at D♭, which is the same sounding pitch as C♯.

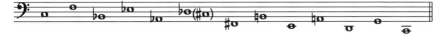

> Notes that sound the same but are written differently, such as C♯ and D♭, are called **enharmonic** equivalents.

In practice, in order to stay within a single key and provide a shorter route back to the tonic, composers prefer an abbreviated version of this progression, which is known as a **diatonic circle of 5ths**. Notice how the use of a falling diminished 5th is used between the subdominant and the leading note to achieve this:

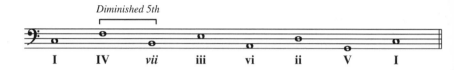

**Common progressions**

Falling 5ths are not the only type of chord sequence that works well. Progressions where the roots fall in 3rds are also very strong and sound good; these are often combined with falling 5ths to create the following well-known chord patterns:

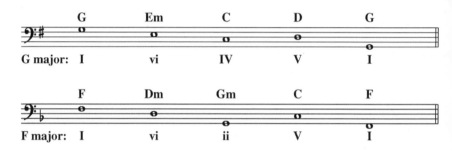

---

## Exercise 8

Refer to your score of the Hornpipe from Handel's *Water Music*. From bar 40 onwards, the second section of the movement contrasts well with the opening key of D major. It is now in the related key of B minor.

1. Identify the chords in bars 40–44¹. Your ears will hear the suspensions in the melody, creating dissonance against the chords, that are then resolved as Handel works through the sequence.

2. In bars 44–48, circle the minim in the bass at the start of each bar and trace the partial circle of 5ths that begins with the dominant note of the key, F♯.

3. From bar 49, we become alerted to the prevailing emphasis on C♯ – a **dominant pedal** that tips us, not into F♯ minor as we might expect at bar 57, but to F♯ major. Trace the circle of 5ths from this point onwards: how is the music different from bars 44–48?

---

**Using second-inversion chords**

Second-inversion chords tend to sound harmonically unstable, as if they want to move on to another chord. This is why a second inversion of chord I (Ic) often precedes a perfect cadence. In a **cadential 6-4** progression, chord Ic falls on the strong beat and the dominant root that follows forms the bass of both Ic and V. Sometimes the second of these repeated bass notes (chord V) drops down an octave, shown by the bracketed note in the next example. This creates the familiar shape shown in the bass part at the cadence:

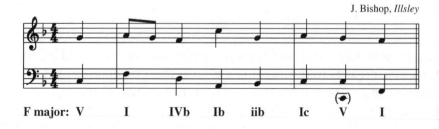

J. Bishop, *Illsley*

A second inversion can also be used when the music passes between the root position and first inversion of the same chord, as shown right. Incidentally, both of these progressions work equally well in reverse: Ib–Vc–I and IVb–Vc–IV. This type of second inversion always comes on the weaker part of the bar and is known as a passing $^6_4$.

G major: I   Vc   Ib      IVb   Ic   IV

Both types of second inversion, passing and cadential, appear in the following example – notice how smoothly the inner parts move:

Traditional, *All Through the Night*

G major: IVb   Ic   IV   Ib   IV   Ic   IVb   vi   ii____ iib   Ic_____ V   I

## Working in full texture

The music of *All Through the Night* (in the previous example), is written in a type of texture commonly found in four-part vocal writing. It is notated on two staves. The melody or soprano part is written on the treble stave with note stems pointing up. Below it is the alto part, written on the same treble stave but with stems pointing down. The tenor part is written on the bass stave with stems pointing up, below which comes the bass part with stems pointing down.

> For the purpose of these exercises, 'full texture' means at least three notes sounding together.

When writing in four-part harmony, at least one note in each triad has to appear twice in the chord in order to produce the required total of four parts. We speak of such notes as being doubled. There are some basic rules of good practice about which notes to double in a chord:

➤ The root is generally the best note to double. Alternatively, the 5th can be doubled (and is often the best option in second inversion chords).

➤ The 3rd of a major triad should not be doubled (doubling the 3rd in other triads is fine).

➤ A chord may contain the root in three of the four parts, as long as the 3rd of the chord is present in the remaining part.

When spacing chords in four-part harmony, note that:

➤ The interval between the soprano and alto, and between the alto and tenor, should never be more than an octave.

➤ The interval between the two lowest parts (tenor and bass) can be more than an octave.

A useful tip for achieving good spacing is to keep the tenor part high. Tenors are used to singing notes up to G above middle C, so don't be afraid to make use of leger lines above the bass stave when writing your tenor parts.

# Exercise 9

attrib. W Croft: *St Anne*

[Musical score: SATB four-part harmony in G major, showing Soprano/Alto on treble staff and Tenor/Bass on bass staff. Chord labels below: ii⁷b ... In G major: V⁷ I]

1. Sing or play through the soprano and bass parts. Notice that they are both more shapely and lyrical, compared to the supporting inner parts (alto and tenor).

2. Make a note of the key and mark in the ends of the phrases. Note that each phrase starts with a crotchet up-beat (anacrusis).

3. Sing the alto line alone. You will notice that it is quite static and avoids large leaps within each phrase.

4. Sing the tenor line alone. It is a little less static than the alto part, but in general avoids large leaps.

5. Indicate the harmonies using Roman numerals. Some chords have been provided for you.

6. Identify the cadences at the end of each phrase.

7. Analyse the relative movement between the soprano and bass parts, using the following descriptions:

   ➢ Contrary motion (moving in opposite directions)

   ➢ Parallel motion (moving in the same direction)

   ➢ Oblique motion (one part moves, the other part remains on the same note).

## Voice leading

Singing, playing and analysing a piece of music written in this type of texture is a practical and interesting way to identify the techniques of four-part harmony.

In traditional harmony, each part should be independent rather than shadowing another. To help create independent parts, it is useful to consider certain types of movement or 'voice leading':

➢ The leading note has a natural pull upwards towards the tonic. In chord V, the 3rd of the chord is the leading note of the scale and so should rise to the tonic in that part

➢ When using chord V⁷, not only should the leading note rise to the tonic, but whichever part has the 7th should fall by step to a note of the next chord, as shown in the cadence at the end of the example used in exercise 9

➢ Avoid moving in parallel intervals (consecutives) of unison, octaves or perfect 5ths between parts, as this type of movement is considered to be weak because the parts do not sound truly independent of each other

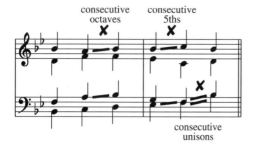

consecutive octaves    consecutive 5ths

consecutive unisons

➢ In the example used in exercise 9, notice how in bar 2¹ the 7th note of chord ii⁷b in the soprano is prepared in the same part in the preceding chord (the C, which is a 3rd in the A minor chord in bar 1⁴).

Traditional rules of harmony state that the 3rd of a major chord should not be doubled, but the 3rd of a minor chord can be doubled. You will notice, however, in bar $1^3$ of the example used in exercise 9, the 3rd of the tonic chord is sounded twice in the alto and bass parts. This is a good example of how a breaking of the 'rule' can be justified on the grounds of a better musical outcome. One solution would have been to put a middle C in the alto part. However, that would have created parallel 5ths between the soprano and alto in bar $1^{2-3}$.

## Doubling

## Chord ii in the minor key

Bach: *Zeuch ein zu deinen Thoren* (final phrase)

Vb    i    vb    VI    ii⁷b    V    V⁷    I

In your second year of study you may specialise in chorale harmonisations in the style of Bach. You may include one or two examples in your submission at AS level. This brief excerpt shows several points of interest for correct voice leading in the minor key.

The cadence combining various possibilities of chords ii, V and I is very common in Bach chorales and is used more frequently than the 6–4 cadence.

Voice leading of chord ii⁷ in the minor key includes correct preparation of the 7th in the alto part by sounding the note in the previous beat. The 7th must then fall. Notice the smooth resolution of this diminished chord with all parts moving by step to chord V, finally resolving to a pleasing conclusion.

Bach permits the 3rd of chord V in the alto part to fall, allowing the full final chord, including the 5th, to be represented. Although this appears to contradict the previous advice that the leading note must rise to the tonic, Bach's resolutions in chorale harmonisations are an exception!

When composing in a minor key, Bach often favours a tonic major chord to end with – known as a *Tierce de Picardie*. In this example, the final chord becomes A major rather than remaining as A minor.

Here are two workings of the third and fourth phrases of the hymn melody used in exercise 9.

Notice the smooth and shapely bass line, using the melodic minor scale version as it descends, avoiding an ugly interval of the augmented 2nd between the second and third quavers of bar 1.

## Comparing two solutions

## Example 1

attrib. W Croft: *St Anne*

In this first example, bar $1^4$ avoids doubling the 3rd of the G major chord, however it creates an awkward leap up to the E in the tenor part. The passing-note quaver in the tenor line of bar 2 appears musical, however it creates parallel 5ths between the tenor and bass from beats 2–3 (the parallel 5ths are identified by grey noteheads).

**Example 2**

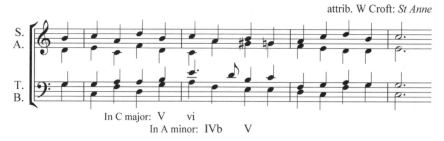

attrib. W Croft: *St Anne*

In C major:   V      vi
In A minor:   IVb     V

In the second example, the doubling of the 3rd in chord V (bar 1⁴) allows for a more satisfying shape in the tenor line. The E sounds first as the 5th degree of chord vi; it then becomes a suspension (bar 2²), prepared on 2¹ and then resolving to become the root of chord IVb, before approaching the imperfect cadence in A minor on beat 3. The overlapping of parts between tenor and alto is entirely justified on the grounds of a 'musical' solution. Alternatively, it would also be possible to put the tenor line in the alto part, but be careful to avoid creating parallel 5ths as you move from V to vi – a common mistake!

**Part writing: summary**

It is good practice to try to conform to the rules of part writing wherever you can. As the examples above show, however, the most important priority is the linear shaping of each vocal line.

It is useful to note that these 'rules' about parallel intervals apply to traditional part-writing. Consecutive parallel octaves are frequently used in piano and orchestral music, and parallel root-position triads (which generate parallel 5ths) are common in modern pop music.

In your coursework exercises you should show an understanding of the way that inner parts connect from one beat to the next, whether the harmony is moving in block chords or in a more linear, melodic style. It is particularly important to observe voice-leading conventions if you choose to submit hymn-melody harmonisations.

## Exercise 10

This exercise uses a traditional melody, with an opening harmonisation given on the guitar. A full texture for a polyphonic instrument such as the guitar should distinguish in the notation between the bass part (stems down) and the inner harmony, using idiomatically notated chords. Complete the remaining three bars.

Traditional English: *The Miller of Dee*

## A complete exercise

This chapter has covered a range of starting points for your exercises. Bearing in mind the list of options mentioned on page 23, the following completed exercise is only one example of many possibilities. The given material is the complete melody plus the whole of the four-bar introduction. The actual working is 16 bars long and is modelled on the three-part texture of the given opening:

The instruction *D.S. al fine* at bar 20 tells the performer to repeat the music from the sign 𝄋 until the word *Fine* in bar 12.

Notice how the bass and chords follow the descending sequence of the melody from bar 13, not deviating from the pattern until bar 18.

There is a **modulation** (change of key) to the dominant (D major) in bars 19–20 of the exercise above, signalled by C♯ in the melody and confirmed by a perfect cadence in the new key.

**Modulation**

The E-minor triad in bar 18 prepares the way for this modulation by acting as a **pivot chord** – a chord that is common to two keys. Here, E minor is chord vi of G major, the key we are leaving, and chord ii of D major, the key we are approaching. Notice how the modulation is shown in the chord symbols. These make it clear how the music has moved from one key to another and how the chord in bar 18 acts as a pivot chord.

You should include at least one or two exercises in your portfolio that show you know how to modulate. Modulations are likely to be to closely related keys, such as the dominant, subdominant or relative minor.

You will need a second modulation in order to return to the tonic. Here, the chord in bar 20 is chord I of D major, but also chord V of G major. It thus prepares the way for the return of the tonic key when the music repeats from bar 5.

**The usefulness of the diminished 7th chord in modulation**

We already know that in any key, the triad built on the 7th degree of the scale sounds quite different because it is a diminished triad. It can be useful to think of this as a dominant 7th triad, without the root as you can see in the example above. By superimposing another 3rd on the dominant chord (major or minor) the chord becomes a dominant 9th chord. Without the root, the dominant minor 9th chord is a vertical stack of minor 3rds and it is called a diminished 7th chord. Because the intervals are equidistant, any one of the four notes can be used as a leading note to resolve to a new chord – very useful in modulation.

## Exercise 11

1.  Examine Handel's *Hornpipe* from bar 18 onwards to see how the composer modulates to the dominant key by bar 27. Remember to transpose the horn parts when you are working out the harmony of each bar.

2.  In the first movement of Beethoven's Symphony No. 5 examine some of the ways the diminished chord is important in moving to a new key.

    ➤ Bar 44: note how the composer moves towards the relative major key of E♭ for the second subject. Complete the table:

| Bar | Harmony | | Description / function |
|---|---|---|---|
| 44–7 | Chord I | C minor | Descending arpeggio, rhythmic motif in bass leads to |
| 48–51$^1$ | | | |
| 51$^2$ | | | |
| 52–56 | | | How does this chord resolve? |
| 57 | rest | | |
| 58 | Chord Vb | | |

    ➤ Construct a similar table to look at other instances of the use of the diminished 7th chord, for example bars 168 and 296.

**An exercise completed under timed conditions**

Towards the end of the course you will complete an exercise without help from your teacher and under supervised conditions. You will be given an hour to do this and you will be able to use an instrument such as a keyboard, guitar or notation software (with any assistance disabled) as you work. The exercise should be of a similar standard to those exercises you have been working on towards the end of the course. You should be able to show that, working independently, you can match your coursework achievement.

# Assessment

Of the 45 marks available for your portfolio:

➤ 20 are awarded for harmonic language (your choice and pacing of chords, and use of effective progressions)

➤ 15 are awarded for technique (creating a strong and well-shaped bass line, continuing the texture from a given opening, identifying and providing the correct working for key changes, and a clear understanding of voice-leading)

➤ 10 are awarded for the clear and accurate use of notation.

The exercise on page 39 should achieve a good mark because:

➤ The bass has a strong shape resulting from the use of primary triads in root position, along with occasional secondary triads and inversions

➤ The inner part moves smoothly, avoiding awkward intervals, and the bass moves largely in contrary motion to the melody

➤ The chord progressions lead effectively to the cadences and include correctly resolved dominant 7ths, appropriate use of chord Ic, modulation and (in bars 13–17) a falling-5ths pattern in which a harmonic sequence (iii–vi$^7$–ii–V$^7$) nicely reflects the melodic sequence in bars 13–16

➤ The work has been checked for good voice leading, with no consecutive (parallel) 5ths or octaves between melody and bass.

Maintaining momentum and a sense of harmonic direction from the start to the end of each phrase is especially important. With experience and observation of how harmony functions in your set works, you will become more confident and successful in the harmonic choices you make.

# Preparing your portfolio

Exercises may be either hand-written, providing they are legible and accurate, or you may use notation software. As this is a coursework unit, the moderator will expect to see your teacher's marks and comments on your work. This helps the moderator to understand the way you have been taught and the understanding you have gained throughout the course. It is often better not to produce neat copies since new mistakes easily creep in when making changes.

Make sure that the given material is clearly identified in each exercise, so that the moderator can see exactly what you have added. Use a highlighter pen or provide a copy of the original template you were given for each exercise.

Remember that it is possible to make mistakes even when using a computer notation programme. Notes of chords in each part must be vertically aligned and notes must have correct accidentals – for example, writing A♭ rather than G♯ is an error if you are in the key of A minor. Correct beaming of grouped notes is also important.

All exercises must include chord symbols – either Roman numerals (with inversion letters) to show the chords, or letter names (with slash chords to show inversions) or figured bass. You should not use guitar tab because this shows finger positions rather than actual pitches, but you can add tab above the stave notation if you find it useful when trying out your work.

Your teacher will assess your portfolio and it will then need to be available for moderation if required. It should be clear to the moderator which of your exercises form the core evidence upon which assessment has been made. It is not necessary for you to include preliminary work. Make sure that access to your exercises is easy; a simple paper clip to group your sheets together is more effective than plastic pockets.

The following checklist can help you make sure that when you select the exercises to include in your portfolio, all requirements for Section A of the composing unit have been met.

## Portfolio checklist

- [ ] At least six dated exercises, completed during the course
- [ ] One further exercise completed under supervision towards the end of the course
- [ ] All exercises contain between 8 and 24 bars of added material
- [ ] Bass line and chord symbols completed in all exercises
- [ ] Bass line, chord symbols *and inner part(s)* completed in at least two full-texture exercises
- [ ] A range of keys represented, with at least one exercise in a minor key
- [ ] Appropriate identification of cadences and cadence approaches
- [ ] Examples that show the appropriate use (and resolution) of chords $V^7$ and $ii^7$
- [ ] Examples showing the appropriate use of second inversions
- [ ] Example(s) including modulation
- [ ] Notation checked for accuracy and legibility

## Section B: Instrumental Techniques

For this part of the unit you can write *either*:

➢ A composition for 4–10 instruments or

➢ An arrangement of a lead sheet for 4–10 instruments.

You should think carefully about the 'brief' you set yourself. This is a concise, short statement in which your basic intention for the arrangement or composition is clearly stated. This may change as your composing work progresses, but it is important to provide this self-determined overview.

Whether you choose a composition or arrangement, you will need to submit a full score of your work in staff notation, the brief, commentary and a recording. You must also submit the original lead sheet if the arrangement option is chosen.

The following information is relevant to both composing and arranging. Your work will be judged by the same criteria, whatever your choice, but some specific issues relating to arrangements are mentioned on page 57.

## Introduction

The area of study, The Expressive Use of Instrumental Techniques, takes centre stage in this part of the composing unit. You will need to understand the characteristics of a range of instruments and the ways in which they can be combined. Your own experience as a performer and your knowledge of the set works will form a good starting point for this. The word 'expressive' in the area of study is of particular importance – in composing we express our thoughts and feelings, sometimes in a surprisingly objective and methodical way, via the medium of a musical instrument. To express is to *communicate*. You must have your audience in mind, if you want to be really successful in communicating your compostitional ideas to potential listeners.

**Which instruments can I use?**

The composition must be for 4–10 instruments, which can be acoustic, amplified or a combination of both. You can include voices if you wish, but only in addition to the 4–10 instruments, and you should note that you can only gain credit for your writing for instruments.

You have a wide choice of instruments (but see right for some important exceptions). However, it makes sense to write for:

> You need to show that you can write for instruments, not their synthesised equivalents. For example, a flute part should be designed to be played on a flute, not a synthesiser. However, you are allowed to use synthetic sounds in the final recording, if necessary. If you and your teacher are unsure what is permissible, contact OCR and ask.

➢ A group of fellow students who will be available to try out your work as it progresses, and to rehearse and perform it for the final recording

➢ A group of instruments that will sound well together.

**How long should the piece be?**

The upper limit is three minutes, but there is no penalty if your work does not precisely meet this requirement. You should aim to say everything you want to say, musically speaking, within this time. Be disciplined and avoid rambling on for longer than necessary, but avoid a piece that is too short as it won't allow you to show the full value of your ideas and range of expertise.

**Style**

You can write in any style you wish, but it is easier to work in an idiom with which you are really familiar. All composers have learned from existing music by playing it, listening to it, studying it and arranging it, only gradually developing their own composing voice. It is important that you too study the music of others as a way of developing your own skill as a composer. In the commentary it is especially important to give details of all the pieces you have studied that are relevant to your composition, and explain precisely how they have informed your work.

**How can I develop aural familiarity?**

Showing that you are familiar with a wide range of music that has played an important and relevant part in your composing activity is essential. As performers and listeners we absorb aspects of music we become familiar with through playing, study and repeated listening. Composers across time have been influenced, consciously or otherwise, by the music around them. Your study of prescribed works in the Introduction to Historical Study in Music unit will help

International Music Score Library Project (http://imslp.org) is a useful source of public domain music. Scores, however, may not always be accurate.

you understand the choices of style, instrumentation and harmonic language that composers have made as they build and develop their musical structures. You will learn about the craft of composition in both a jazz and classical context.

You will need to explain the relevance of your listening to the shaping of your ideas. It is expected that you will draw on your personal listening and study as well as the prescribed works and recordings.

> Create a chart to show the variety and extent of music you know and admire. What gaps are there you might want to explore?

> Borrow scores of your favourite pieces from libraries or download them from the internet. Identify and copy out melodies, riffs, motifs, rhythms or chord progressions that are interesting. Keep a journal of your discoveries.

> Talk about the range of music available for your instrument or voice with your specialist teacher if you have one. What are the features of successful writing for your instrument/voice?

> Do you play in a small ensemble, band or orchestral group? What ideas for *your* composing might you pick from this experience? Think about forming your own small group to experiment with composing ideas or perform arrangements of interesting music.

**How is your composing assessed?**

The 45 marks available for your composition or arrangement are split into four categories, each of which will be explored in detail over the following pages:

> **Materials (10 marks)** are your basic ideas, the building blocks of your piece such as rhythmic patterns, melodies, bass parts and chord progressions, together with a clear account in your commentary of the listening that has influenced the shaping of these materials

> **Use of medium (15 marks)** refers to your understanding of the particular qualities of the instruments you have used and the ways in which you have combined them

> **Technique (10 marks)** is the skill with which your materials have been constructed on a small scale and then developed, combined and connected to form a larger structure

> **Communication (10 marks)** is the way in which you have conveyed your ideas in both the score (which needs to be complete and accurate) and the recording (which needs to give an effective interpretation/performance of your music).

As there is no restriction on the style of your work, remember that the examples given in the rest of this chapter indicate only some of the possibilities open to you.

## Materials

**Melodic materials**

One of the most important elements in many types of music is melody. Your work in Section A of this unit will help you to understand the various ways in which melodies can be constructed.

The melodies you are using will be by established composers; as you perform them, they will provide you with good models of small-scale structure. The character of a melody is shaped by its rhythm, pitches, overall contour and pace. Strong melodies often consist of mainly stepwise movement with occasional leaps. Think about the opening of the well-known tune *Greensleeves* – the melodic intervals reflect this basic principle and we can also hear that the leaps are ones with strong harmonic implications (chord notes are marked *):

The linear intervals created as a melody moves from one note to the next can have a profound effect on its character. John Williams' theme for *Schindler's List* is deeply expressive whether or not we know the subject matter of the film. Another melody, Beethoven's *Ode to Joy* has a somewhat measured and noble quality. Consider the extent to which these characteristics are related to the use of stepwise and angular movement within the melodies.

Both pitch and rhythm play a part in determining the character of a melody as can be heard in Henry Mancini's *Pink Panther* theme:

Even when melodies are not particularly distinctive in either pitch or rhythm, we can see invention in the way they unfold. Notice how the melody of the folk song *The Water is Wide* (below) slowly expands the range of notes outlined in each of its four phrases. There is a firm sense of upward direction in the unfolding melody as it moves toward the high point at bar 9 before finally coming to rest in the fourth phrase:

The climax of a melody is often found between two-thirds and three-quarters of the way through, as in the example below. It doesn't have to be loud, highpitched and joyous – it could be low, quiet and mysterious.

A good way to write a melody is to start with a short, memorable **motif** which can be repeated, manipulated or contrasted to form a phrase. More importantly, such motifs can become a source for development in different ways later in the piece.

A short motif can exert a powerful presence: think about the opening of Beethoven's Symphony No. 5 or the mambo bell pattern of Gillespie's *Manteca*. Sometimes melodic fragments can be woven into a textural fabric that forms the basis for a whole work. This can be seen in the work of composers such as Steve Reich, Michael Nyman and John Adams.

The next example is built on a four-note motif. When the motif is repeated, its opening interval (an octave) contracts to a 7th. The second half of the phrase starts with another repetition of the motif (in which the opening interval is now reduced to a 5th), but this time the motif is extended to eight crotchet beats in length, thus balancing the combined length of its first two appearances. The graph-like lines above the stave show the contour of the melody, which consists of a long descent to balance the upward leaps at the start of the motif:

[Allegro]                                    Bach, Orchestral Suite No. 3 in D, Gavotte I

---

## Exercise 12

1. Construct a balanced melody of four phrases in an inverted arch shape ( ⌣ ) in which the lowest point is reached in the third phrase. Base it on a short motif that is modified and then extended to provide contrast. The previous two music examples are good models of this.

2. In your study of the set works, you will notice that composers frequently shape melodic materials using stepwise movement, arpeggios or repeated notes. Compare the opening 8-bar horn melody in Mozart's Concerto K. 495 with the melody of the violin/oboe at the start of Handel's Trumpet Minuet HWV 349/13.

3. There are other pitch configurations in addition to the major and minor scales used in the orchestral set works. Find out about alternative modes such as Dorian and Lydian. Explore the pitch patterns of other cultures, for example Arabic or Balinese. Write out some melodic ideas using these various 'modes'.

4. Investigate the ways in which motifs are used and distinctive themes constructed in as many of the following works as possible:

   ➢ Delius: 'La Calinda' from *Three Orchestral Pieces*

   ➢ Bizet: 'Farandole' from *L'Arlésienne* Suite No. 2

   ➢ Grieg: 'Morning Mood' and 'In the Hall of the Mountain King' from *Peer Gynt* Suite

   ➢ Bartók: Concerto for Orchestra, third movement

   ➢ Reich: Three Movements for Orchestra (1986), second movement.

---

**Bass materials**

We have already noted in Section A (page 31) that bass notes underpin the harmonic possibilities of a piece of music. A bass part may have a strongly melodic character, as found in music of a **contrapuntal** texture where each of the voices has an independent line. In rock music, **riffs** in the bass part can play an important role too; they may be the foundation upon which an entire piece is built.

A **ground bass** is a repeating bass part above which different melodies unfold. While it is a device often associated with Baroque music, it can be very effective in other styles of music. Pachelbel's well-known Canon in D is built upon a simple ground bass that is played 28 times, while a series of increasingly complex melodies unfold in canon above it. Other examples to study include the Ricercare from Bach's *Musical Offering*, Britten's Passacaglia from *Peter Grimes* and *When God Created the Coffee Break* from the album *Strange Place for Snow* by the Esbjörn Svensson Trio.

Clearly notated examples of typical walking, rock and Latin bass lines (and idiomatic drum patterns) can be found in *Jazz Styles: History and Analysis* by Mark C. Gridley. Pearson, 11th edition, 2011. ISBN 978-0-20503683-7.

Your study of jazz recordings will allow you to investigate a range of bass lines and their relationship to the harmonic framework. You may have studied the 12-bar blues for GCSE and now at AS level you will learn how standard bass patterns can be presented in various interesting ways to suit 8-, 16-, 20- and 32-bar structures.

A weakness in many AS compositions is a bass part that doesn't go beyond simply reinforcing the harmony and so lacks real interest in its own right. Yet, in an iconic work like Miles Davis' *So What*, the bass player is entrusted with the most important motivic material from the start. In addition to the good practice you will find in the orchestral scores and jazz recordings you study, the music of the following bass players may be instructive:

➤ Ray Brown

➤ Jaco Pastorius (Weather Report and solo)

➤ Michael 'Flea' Balzary (Red Hot Chili Peppers)

➤ Esperanza Spalding.

## Exercise 13

Using a good quality pair of headphones, listen to Paul Chambers' bass playing in the recording of 'Round Midnight. Make a detailed analysis using a chart with timings/structural landmarks to identify the various types of playing that Chambers uses in the recording. Listen for scalic patterns, leaps, chromatic movement, rhythmic emphasis, slides, and playing that is supportive of the other musicians and that which is more independent.

**Rhythmic materials**

Rhythm is a key ingredient in establishing the character of a piece. Steady crotchets, robotic quavers, lilting triplets, snappy dotted rhythms, lively syncopations, rapid semiquavers or asymmetric patterns such as those created by the heavy string accents in Stravinsky's *Rite of Spring* – each can create a different mood.

Dance-based music is usually associated with particular rhythmic patterns and regular phrase lengths: slow duple time for stately pavans, fast compound time for jigs, moderate triple time for waltzes, duple-time phrases that begin halfway through the bar for gavottes (as in the example on page 46) and so on.

The Latin music associated with the countries of South America has enjoyed great popularity in a variety of musical contexts. For example, several of the numbers in Bernstein's *West Side Story* (1957) are based on Latin-American dances. Such influences have been heard in popular music and jazz for many decades. More recently, the work of the Cuban ensemble *Buena Vista Social Club* contributed to a revival of interest in Latin-American music. The continuing success of artists such as Shakira and Carlos Santana (who released *Supernatural* – the hugely successful album produced in collaboration with younger artists) is convincing proof that its popularity continues.

African drumming and Balinese gamelan as well as the music of the medieval French composer Pérotin have influenced the music of Steve Reich. The compositions of Philip Glass and Peter Gabriel's film scores similarly show the rhythmic influences of other times and cultures. The short works listed right provide further fruitful opportunities to experience ostinati and driving rhythms at work.

Remember that your initial rhythmic ideas will need refinement and control as you continue to work on your composition.

John Adams: *Short Ride in a Fast Machine*

Louis Andriessen: Instrumental III from *M is for Man, Music, Mozart*

Astor Piazzolla: *Buenos Aires Hora Cero*

It can be productive to consider: working with more unusual time signatures; composing using a changing pulse; subdividing the pulse into unpredictable rhythmic groupings. The following works provide excellent examples to listen to:

> The waltz-like second movement in $\frac{5}{4}$ of Tchaikovsky's Symphony No. 6 in B minor

> *Take Five* written in $\frac{5}{4}$ time and *Unsquare Dance* in $\frac{7}{4}$ time, both performed by The Dave Brubeck Quartet

> The subdivisions within the crotchet pulse of Radiohead's *Pyramid Song*

> Bulgarian Rhythm (113, 115), from Bartók's *Mikrokosmos* Vol. IV for Solo Piano.

**Harmonic materials**

If you write in a tonal idiom you will have a feast of listening materials on which to draw, including and beyond the set works. But there are other ways to organise pitch such as serial or nonserial atonality and modality. Most popular music is either tonal or modal, and so beginning with a chord progression is often a good starting point for many student composers.

Listen to Barber's *Adagio for Strings* and excerpts from Michael Nyman's film scores for examples in which the harmonic materials dominate the musical content. For both these composers, the richness of their harmonic language is influenced by music of the Baroque and Classical periods. Nyman openly acknowledges his borrowings from Purcell and Mozart.

You will learn in your study of the set works how the organisation of pitch is closely connected with the musical structure. The keys or tonal centres often provide an important means of defining a section, which may move on to develop initial ideas or provide a complete contrast.

### Exercise 14

1.  Research some characteristic rhythms of dance music from a different culture. Compose a short piece of 16–20 bars for two instruments that incorporate your findings.

2.  Listen to extracts from Nyman's 'Chasing sheep is best left to shepherds' (from *The Draughtsman's Contract*) or Overture and Serenata from Stravinsky's *Pulcinella*. In these works, both composers write in a pastiche Baroque style but with a modern sound.

3.  Compose a short chord sequence of your own for keyboard or guitar using a single harmonic figuration. Create a complementary melody for an instrument of your choice.

## Use of medium

Marks in this category are awarded for how well you have written for the instruments you have used – are the parts playable and do they exploit the character of the instrument? Is there interest in all of the parts – or are some condemned to dull accompaniment patterns with little melodic interest?

In preparation, you will need to research all you can about the instruments you use. Discuss with the performers: the various tone colours available at different dynamics; any special effects that might be possible; how much time is needed to insert a mute or take a breath on a wind instrument; which chords are possible on a guitar; which musical features (such as glissandos, trills or fast passages involving low notes) might prove difficult; what different types of tonguing, bowing or vibrato sound like, and so on.

Will your composition be written for a small group of soloists: a brass quartet; a string quartet with saxophone or electric guitar, for example? Or you may wish to compose for a small chamber orchestra – a string section with wind soloists or tuned percussion perhaps. In your composition for between four and ten instruments, note the following:

➤ a section of violins counts as one part

➤ a full string section of Violins I, II, Viola, Cello and Double Bass represents 5 parts.

You should make it clear in your commentary if you are writing solo string parts or for a larger string section with more than one instrument per part.

When researching the capabilities of the instruments you intend to use, remember that there are many sources of advice:

➤ The performers you are going to use and any specialist tutors who may teach in your school or college

➤ The classical and jazz set works you are studying, which include many examples of good practice

➤ Books such as those listed in the box on the right

➤ Internet sites, such as www.bbc.co.uk/orchestras/guide/, www.soundjunction.org ('instruments and voices' section) and www.nyphilkids.org ('instrument storage room' section) – the last of these is aimed at children but all three include detailed examples and useful factual information.

*Orchestral Technique: A Manual for Students* by Gordon Jacob. Oxford University Press, 1931/1982, ISBN 978-0-193182-04-2.

*Orchestration* by Cecil Forsyth. Dover Publications, 1914/1986, ISBN 978-0-486243-83-2.

*Rock, Jazz and Pop Arranging* by Daryl Runswick. Faber Music, 1993, ISBN 978-0-571511-08-2.

## Orchestration: what can I learn from the prescribed scores?

An excellent way to learn about orchestration – how to compose for different instruments – is to look at the example of skilled composers, studying and getting to know plenty of scores. You are expected to understand the idiomatic qualities of the instruments you write for, both as 'solo' voices and in ensemble textures where they are combined with other instruments.

The string section features strongly in Western orchestral music. Even though we are used to hearing synthesised strings in popular and ambient music, for the purposes of your composing it is the original acoustic instrument that you must have in mind. If you are used to composing at a computer or a keyboard, a common mistake is to write parts that are 'pianistic' but unsuitable or even impossible for a stringed instrument to play.

**Writing for strings and winds**

While it is important to know the range of notes that each of your chosen instruments play, in reality there is much more to know than simply the highest and lowest note. The quality of sound can vary considerably in different areas of an instrument's range. For example:

> ➤ an oboe is difficult to play quietly in the lower three or four notes of its range

> ➤ a flute is comparatively quiet in its lower octave; it is at its brightest and most penetrating when written on leger lines

> ➤ the clarinet has a wonderfully rich lower chalumeau register – quite different to its timbre higher in the range

> ➤ it is easy to forget that the bassoon, cello and trombone are equivalent to a 'tenor' vocal role and can be written for effectively in the higher register, often notated in the tenor clef.

The violin is considered one of the most expressive of instruments. When writing for strings it is useful to have a simple understanding of the open strings and finger positions so that you can appreciate some of the types of figuration that are possible, including double and triple stopping, and 4-note chords. The strings are tuned in perfect 5ths – ask a violinist to show you the relative placement of the fingers on the strings in various positions.

First position fingerings for all the 'natural' notes on the violin:

Beethoven: Symphony No. 5, *Allegro con brio*

Bowing techniques include the use of down-bow movement (⊓) and up-bow (⋁). It is not necessary to use these signs very much on your composing score because the players will write them in – a down-bow on a strong beat, the up-bow often for an anacrusis opening to a phrase. The use of slurs and phrase marks are, however, very important to indicate what bowing is required. A slur indicates the number of notes to be played in a single bow stroke. These markings show how to articulate the music – for a wind player it is by the use of the tongue, for a string player a similar effect is achieved by control of the bow.

The slurring in the following string passage of Beethoven's Fifth Symphony gives the melody as much of its character as the pitches and rhythm:

Here is an example of what might be learned from the opening of the Allegro in Handel's *Water Music*. Technically there are 13 instrumental parts here – your own composition needs to be three instruments fewer.

| Bar | Instrument(s) | Description | Significance |
| --- | --- | --- | --- |
| 1 onwards | Bass | No distinction between cello and double bass; both would be present, sounding an octave apart | Common practice in Baroque period |
| 1 | Woodwind/strings | Full tonic chord including bass | Strong opening but keeping the brass sound in reserve for the fanfare-like motif to follow |
| 2–5 | Upper/mid strings only | Descending scales in unison | Unison/octaves: this is a useful, strong texture |
| | Oboes | | Oboes often double violin 1 |
| 1–5 | 2 trumpets | Energetic, harmonic fanfare motif | Creates a bright festive opening |
| 5–9 | 2 horns | Fanfare response | *Contrast* of timbre: now mellow brass sound and accompanied by bassoon and bass only |
| 9–13 | Strings | Upper strings return | Some harmony |
| | | Bass punctuates | Emphasis on tonic/dominant |
| | Woodwind | Oboes in 3rds, then joins violin 1 | Add brightness to the trumpets |
| | | | Note the C♯ on the oboe at bar 13 – the only instrument on the 3rd of the chord |
| | | Bassoon | Supports string bass |
| 13–15 | Horns, bassoon, bass | Horns respond to the previous trumpet call | Reduced instrumentation again provides contrast |
| 15–19 | Oboes, upper strings | Oboe does not quite mirror upper string octaves | Oboe shaped *into* the cadence at bars 18-19 |
| | | | The accompaniment gives an unobtrusive 'frame' for the bright, dotted trumpet pattern |
| 19–23 | Horns, bassoon, bass | Horns continue to match the upper register of the trumpet with an echo of the pattern | Note how the bassoon and bass part company at the cadence |

In this approach, observation of everything going on happens bar by bar. It is really important to be observant about all the orchestration decisions a composer makes, but also to ask the question 'Why?'.

Another approach is to use a log or diary to note particularly striking use of instruments. This could lead on to more detailed investigation.

| Beethoven Symphony No. 5, Allegro con brio | | |
|---|---|---|
| **Location** | **Instruments** | **Of interest …** |
| Exposition | Strings/Full orchestra | Comparing the effect of the opening motif in bar 1 instrumentation with bar 22 |
| | Woodwind and horn role in sustained notes | |
| | Timpani and lower strings | Powerful effect of repeated quavers in bar 52 |
| | Horn alone, bar 59 | Passing the melody – violins – clarinet – violins doubled at the octave by flute |
| | Viola and double bass | Creeping ascending chromaticism in bar 84 |
| Bar 110 | Woodwind and horn | The horn is used to add 'body' to the descending arpeggios |
| Bar 182 | Low to higher wind | Dark to light timbres in ascending figure |
| Bar 217 | 6-note woodwind chords – higher register | Played *sempre più* ***p*** sounds really delicate |
| Bar 268 | Oboe | Plaintive, decorative quality of the oboe played entirely alone as a 'pause' before the music continues as before |

You might want to continue to make a complete table in this format.

**Exercise 15**

1. In the first movement of Beethoven's Symphony No. 5, study the first violin part from bar 94 in terms of the bowing and articulation marks. Think through (or mime) the up-bow and down-bow strokes that a performer would use.

2. Find a passage in music that you play on your own instrument where the articulation is essential to the character of the idea. Share your findings with other instrumentalists.

3. In the Rondo in Mozart's Horn Concerto K. 495 make a thorough investigation of the way the notes of the harmony are distributed among the string players. Notice how the 'voice leading' is attended to so that each instrument has a well-shaped linear part to play.

**What can I learn from listening to other music?** It is expected that you will learn about instrumentation from listening more widely than just your prescribed works. Here are some suggestions to broaden your understanding of the ways composers use instruments in a range of different compositions.

**String quartet listening** In addition to the body of Classical quartets written by Haydn and Mozart, there are many compositional discoveries to be made in each of the quartets composed in the early 20th century by Ravel and Debussy, and the group of six quartets composed by Bartók.

Techniques demonstrated in these works include: *con sordini* (play 'with the mute'); the use of harmonics, tremolo between non-adjacent notes, various bowing sonorities such as *sul ponticello* (play 'near the bridge') and *col legno* (play 'with the wood' of the bow), in addition to extreme pizzicato techniques such as snapping the string against the fingerboard. The pizzicato chords of the second movement of Debussy's String Quartet in G minor (alternating with the quasi-Spanish melodic line) produce a stylised guitar effect.

It can be rewarding to study works that correspond more closely to the size of forces you may use yourself. A number of famous composers such as Ravel, Mussorgsky and Stravinsky worked initially at the piano and later orchestrated their ideas, as well as producing piano or piano duet versions of their compositions.

➤ A comparison of the piano version of the Minuet from Ravel's *Le Tombeau de Couperin* with the orchestral version reveals some highly idiomatic wind scoring.

➤ Schubert's Octet (clarinet, bassoon, horn, 1st and 2nd violins, viola, cello and double bass) provides valuable instruction on instruments playing individually for their specific timbre, or collectively in textures to which small groups of instruments or the whole ensemble contribute.

➤ Brass instruments and timpani are treated with invention and dramatic flair in the exciting opening movement of Janacek's Sinfonietta.

In all the music you listen to, pay attention to the ways in which composers move from one idea to another, smoothly or suddenly. There is often a link. Make note of the techniques used to avoid losing pace in a piece, such as the overlapping of sections, or a clear sense of harmonic direction as the music moves towards a high point or moves away.

## Smaller chamber works

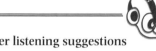

**Further listening suggestions**

'Dodge The Dodo' from *Love Is Real* by Ulf Wakenius. Listen to the way the first violin takes the role of the drum kit in this arrangement.

A great many 'extended' string techniques associated with avant-garde music can be heard in works such as Penderecki's *Threnody to the Victims of Hiroshima* and George Crumb's *Black Angels*. You may wish to make use of them in an appropriate stylistic context, but don't forget that more standard techniques can offer a huge amount of variety.

Many of the scores mentioned here are in the public domain: you can find them on http://imslp.org.

## Exercise 16

Undertake a thorough investigation of an instrument you would like to include in your composition. Use a range of resources including books, scores and the internet; be sure to listen to some of the music that will be recommended in the sources you use. Prepare a five-minute presentation for other students, including a practical demonstration if you have researched an instrument that you play yourself.

## Technique

Marks for technique are awarded for small-scale structures (the way that phrases are organised) and for the form of the entire composition. In both cases, the key to success is to balance unity with variety – too many new or unconnected ideas and your piece will not seem integrated; too much repetition and it risks becoming uninteresting and predictable.

**Large-scale structure**

The examples in the prescribed scores show a range of large-scale structures. Handel uses smaller movements to build a larger picture; many of the movements are in binary form. Mozart skilfully constructs a well-crafted movement combining the balanced phrases of the horn melody on the small-scale with an expansive larger-scale framework allowing for a significant detour into the relative minor key. Beethoven presents us with a structure on a rather larger scale, but gives the impression of compression of ideas presented in a profound context.

Bear in mind the intention of your piece. For example, minimalist or dance music is designed to be repetitive and may not give you much opportunity to show the range of skills required in a three-minute piece. The structure of a film score is often dictated by the action on screen and may not make much musical sense beyond the context of the film.

It is important not to be over-ambitious in a composition of three minutes' duration – simple structures often work best. In ternary form (ABA) the middle section should offer a contrast but should not sound like a totally different piece. When the A section returns, resist the temptation to 'cut and paste' the opening bars. Consider how it can be modified to create a convincing conclusion, aiming for a structure such as ABA[1], perhaps adding a short coda as well.

Some students warm to the idea of a pre-imposed structure such as theme and variation, but nevertheless it is also as well to remember Sondheim's maxim 'Content dictates form'.

**Small-scale structure**

You will know from your study of the materials presented within the prescribed scores that one compositional tool is to build melodies from short balanced units, often two or four bars in length. These motifs are balanced because they are of equal length and are often arranged in complementary pairs (questions and answers).

The opening horn solo in Mozart's Rondo makes this point very clearly.

While the quaver anacrusis 'launches' each phrase and is a recognisable characteristic of the melody, Mozart provides enough by way of surprise and variety to keep the listener alert. It is useful to observe too how Mozart fragments and perpetuates the suspense, before a return to the playfulness of the solo idea presented at bar 38.

Above all, take note of the 'seeds' of ideas that composers present, and the way they 'grow' their carefully formed ideas rather than producing new, unconnected material.

## Exercise 17

Evaluate the small-scale structure of some melodies you are working with in Section A of the composing unit and of some of the melodies you play in your favourite pieces.

Creating music from a few tiny melodic cells can be one of the most fruitful ways of composing, since they offer the potential for development in all sorts of ways, both later in the phrase and later in the piece. Composers have often used standard techniques to enable a melodic idea to grow from the briefest of starting points. Motifs are often repeated before being transformed in some way. Possible transformations include:

| | |
|---|---|
| Transposition | Moving the motif uniformly to a new key |
| Tonal sequence | Repeating the motif at a higher or lower pitch but adapting intervals to stay in the same key |
| Interval alteration | Keeping the general shape but reducing or enlarging the size of some intervals |
| Fragmentation | Using just part of the motif |
| Extension | Continuing the motif beyond its previous end |
| Decoration | Replacing notes with several shorter notes |
| Simplification | Replacing several short notes with a single long note |
| Inversion | Reversing the direction of all the intervals: e.g. rising 3rds become falling 3rds |
| Augmentation | Systematically increasing the length of notes |
| Diminution | Systematically reducing the length of notes |

**Developing ideas**

Motif:

Transposition:

Motif repeated in sequence:

Interval alteration:

Fragmentation:

Extension:

Decoration:

Simplification:

Inversion:

## Exercise 18

1. Identify and explain the ways in which contrasting ideas contribute to the musical structure of a piece you are currently playing or singing.

2. Analyse the structure of a popular song of your choice and show how the form used might be adapted for instrumental composition.

3. Invent a short motif that has the potential to be transformed in some of the ways listed in the table above and then use some of these methods to turn it into a complete theme.

Other techniques include retrograde, in which the order of the notes is reversed (so G–B–C–G–F–E becomes E–F–G–C–B–G ) and retrograde inversion, in which the notes of the retrograde version are also inverted. However, these types of transformation are not easily perceived by the listener, and tend to be used mainly in particular styles of music such as serialism and sometimes minimalism.

Composers frequently combine different types of transformation – so a motif might be fragmented and then that fragment might be used in sequence, inverted and decorated.

What this all boils down to is that you really don't need many ideas for a well-integrated composition – it is what you do with them that counts!

## Communication

When your composition reaches an audience, the process of musical communication will be complete. A written score enables your work to be performed by others and a recording will provide one possible representation of your work in audio format.

### The Score

The layout of the score should follow accepted conventions – refer to published scores to check standard practice. Accuracy of pitch and rhythm are essential. If you use notation software check that the correct clefs have been used to avoid unnecessary leger lines, that key signatures and accidentals are correct, that short notes are beamed correctly and that long notes are not confusingly expressed as multiple tied notes. Find out how to set a small but readable stave size for the score in order to minimise page turns and avoid wasting paper. Check that notes on leger lines don't overlap with the staves above or below.

Make sure that you add full performance directions, including dynamics, phrasing, articulation, marks of expression and tempo directions. Piano pedalling marks and essential bowing marks on string parts could also be relevant to your score. These markings not only increase the likelihood that performers will play your piece as you want them to, but they will also provide evidence that you have thought about the varied ways you can use the instruments to the full in your composition.

Check that the staves have been labelled with instrument names, and give your piece a meaningful title which accurately reflects your intentions.

### Improvisation

If any sections of your composition use improvisation they should at least be notated in outline. Non-notated improvisation by any performer other than the composer is not credited as composition. In a jazz-style context, for example, you should always provide an outline for any improvised material – even if there is some deviation from it in performance.

### The recording

There are various options for recording your composition:

➤ A live performance with intended forces – while this takes time to rehearse and record, it can offer the most realistic realisation of your ideas in most styles of music

➤ A multi-tracked performance in which the various parts are recorded separately and then mixed down into a stereo format

---

### Extending your listening

You can gain some free access to music tracks using websites and applications such as Spotify, and the range of quality performances posted on YouTube is improving all the time.

Use a library: CDs, DVDs and scores are often available for loan from public libraries and possibly from your school or college. Some libraries offer free access to resources such as the thousands of tracks in the Naxos Music Library.

Use the radio: *Late Junction* on Radio 3 offers an eclectic mix of global music, new classical and jazz. *Hear and Now* is the main contemporary music programme on Radio 3. Listen to *Composer of the Week*. Classic FM offers a wide selection of enjoyable, largely mainstream classical repertoire.

Many individual music tracks can be purchased cheaply via internet sites.

Support live musicians by going to concerts in your local area.

---

Note that guitar tablature cannot be offered as an alternative to staff notation. Proficiency in the use of staff notation is a requirement at AS level.

---

Note that it is perfectly acceptable to submit a handwritten score for your final document. Accuracy, legibility and attention to detail are the main issues whichever format you adopt.

➢ A mixture of intended instruments and substitutions for any that are unavailable, such as playing a double-bass part on a synthesiser

➢ A performance on the piano or other keyboard instrument – this means playing from a piano reduction of the score that will usually omit some of the detail

➢ A sequenced version of the composition – this should be fully edited to represent the expressive intentions as effectively as possible

➢ A mixture of sequenced and live parts – even the inclusion of just one live instrument can transform the often mechanical realisation produced by music software.

Don't worry if your live performance contains some mistakes, as this is preferable to a perfect but bland computer recording that does not convey any life or expression.

It makes sense to consider your options right from the earliest planning days of your composition. If you write for fellow students you will be able to try things out as your ideas develop as well as getting valuable advice from the players themselves. You can use other students, teachers and friends to perform your piece if you wish. You do not have to play in your own composition, but you do have to take charge of the rehearsals and recording; after all, this is part of the assessment and so needs to be your own work.

Check your recording on a conventional playback system and keep backup copies of both the recording and the score. You should not submit data files or use other formats which require specialist equipment or programmes. When you hand in your final folio for assessment, you should include your individual recording for your teacher to listen to and assess.

## Arrangement of a lead sheet

If you choose to submit an arrangement instead of a composition you must include a copy of the lead sheet containing the melody and harmony indications with your final submission. The assessment will focus on what you have *added* to this given material and the way in which it has been manipulated and creatively presented. Note that much of the information in the preceding sections is as relevant to arranging as it is to composing.

Many arrangers will have specific jazz or band line-ups for the realisation of their ideas but less conventional uses of medium are also possible and acceptable. Issues for consideration include:

Variety of texture: try to avoid an obvious succession of solos and think about how different pairings or groups of instruments might feature. Try to be imaginative in inventing suitable parts for the rhythm section, especially the bass.

➢ **Melodic additions**: these could include countermelodies, riffs and fills between phrases.

➢ **Melodic alteration**: such as adapting a theme to a different style or using anticipations and syncopation to energise the theme.

**Further listening suggestions**

*Cannonball Adderley's Fiddler on the Roof*. Capitol Jazz 542309-2. This includes arrangements of eight numbers from the hit Broadway show.

John Coltrane: *My Favorite Things*. Atlantic 1361-2. A legendary reworking of a song from Rodger and Hammerstein's *The Sound of Music*.

The Bad Plus: *These are the Vistas*. Columbia 510666-2. Two tracks are described as deconstructions of enormous hits: *Heart of Glass* and *Smells like Teen Spirit*.

> ➤ **Harmonic realisation**: not just voicing the given chords but also varying the harmonies with added notes and substitutions.

> ➤ **Structure**: be imaginative in extending standard structures by adding extra material – an introduction, an ending, interesting features in short solos, new sections that complement the style of the given material.

> ➤ **Instrumentation**: ensure that you use your chosen instruments in an idiomatic way, exploiting their possibilities to the full.

> ➤ **Tempo and key**: consider altering the original and varying the key and/or tempo at some stage in the arrangement.

An example of a form you can use for this can be found in Appendix D1 of the specification.

It is important to supplement your listening with arrangements that are relevant to the style and techniques you have chosen for *your* arrangement. Be aware of the difference between instrumentation and arranging. In the latter there will be strong evidence of creative interpretation of the lead sheet. You should aim to infuse the spirit of the music with your own individual fingerprint as an arranger.

## The commentary and the brief

You will need to give details of your composing brief and provide a commentary about your work. This information shows how you tackled your work and, if done well, can help maximise your marks.

The brief is a concise statement of your composing intentions and you will find it very helpful to discuss ideas with your teacher. The statement may need to be adjusted as work on your composition progresses. Being open to the twists and turns of the creative process may mean your definitive brief will only be certain once the work is well under way.

The purpose of the commentary is to provide:

> ➤ An outline of the *specific pieces* you have listened to and the ways in which they influenced your composing

> ➤ An explanation of the processes you used to create the work.

Try to be very clear about the way in which listening connects with your composition – you may want to use short notated snippets of music in your description to explain this.

You may find it useful to keep a log of your listening research as you go along, to remind you of all that you discover and its relevance to your work.

Simply saying something like 'I really liked the sound of the violin (or guitar) in piece X so I decided to write for this instrument' is not very helpful. It is much more informative to say something along the lines of 'I really liked the sound of the violin in the first movement of Bartók's String Quartet No. X, in particular the extended techniques in the use of the bow such as ...' (and then supply the details), or 'The sound of the lead guitar in Satriani's album *Crystal Planet* opened my eyes to a range of timbres and playing techniques ...' (and then give precise details).

When describing your composing process, try to avoid giving a blow-by-blow account of what is clearly self-evident in the score. A simple, analytical explanation of the main ingredients of your work is important, as is an explanation of the decisions you made about structure, repetition, contrast and so on. Concentrate on explaining *what* you did and, more importantly, *why* you did it.

Spend time on the commentary and aim to show that you are familiar with a range of relevant listening that has influenced your work. Remember that the commentary will provide evidence to the examiner that will help them decide the marks you get for Materials.

## Finally

Whether you are a composer or arranger, take pride in being the author of something that is your very own. Be sure to recognise the fine line between unacceptable plagiarism and legitimate, acknowledged instruction from others. Give yourself plenty of time to rework your ideas; you may need to produce several versions of an idea before you get it right. Take the advice of performers around you and work with instruments from the very start of the composing process if you can. You have many options and must give yourself time to consider carefully the choices you make as the work progresses. If a live performance is a realistic possibility for you, enjoy the sense of achievement that such an opportunity brings. If you are able to add a live element to a technologically realised portrayal of your work you may find this can also be very satisfying. Allow time for rehearsal, revisions, and unanticipated technical problems. Above all, take responsibility for a written and audio representation of your work that expresses your musical ideas with accuracy, clarity and integrity.

# Introduction to historical study in music

## Exam overview

The examination for this unit takes the form of a written paper that lasts for two hours (15 minutes preparation time and 1¾ hours writing time). The question paper is accompanied by a separate booklet (called an 'insert') containing scores and a CD of recorded extracts of music. You are allowed to play the recordings as many times as you wish, within the time available, on a personal CD player equipped with headphones. The paper is in three parts:

### Section A (30 marks)

You will be asked several short aural questions based on two or three recorded passages from a piece of *instrumental* music. The music will not be taken from your set works – it may well be from a piece that you are unfamiliar with. You choose extracts from *either* the period 1700–1830 *or* from popular music from 1900 to the present day. You are advised not to spend more than 40 minutes on this section.

### Section B (40 marks)

There will be two groups of questions:

> The first group is based on a recorded extract and score from *one* of the three orchestral set works that you will have studied (**25 marks**)

> The second group is based on one of the three jazz recordings that you will have studied (**15 marks**).

You must study both sets of music. The detailed list for each year is shown on page 69. Check this carefully to make sure you study the right works for the year that you intend to take the examination.

### Section C (20 marks)

You will have to write an essay in answer to a question on an aspect of the background to one or more of the six set works that you have studied. There will be three questions for you to choose from. Although you only have to answer one question, some of the questions are likely to require writing about more than one of the works.

You are allowed 15 minutes at the start of the examination to read through the paper, look at the scores for Sections A and B, find the tracks on the CD and get yourself organised. Most importantly, this gives you a chance to *listen to all your extracts* – make the most of this opportunity.

Practice questions for Sections A and B of the paper are provided in *OCR AS Music Listening Tests*, 4th edition, by Veronica Jamset and Huw Ellis-Williams (Rhinegold, 2013). ISBN 978-1-78305-224-0.

# Content

The study of any sort of history involves gathering evidence, establishing facts and interpreting them. Music history is no different: it depends on analysing evidence.

**Evidence**

Evidence includes contemporary documents (that is, documents from the day) such as newspaper advertisements, reports and reviews, letters, such as those to or from the composer or others involved in a first performance, bills, records of fees paid to performers or instrument makers, and the diaries and journals of informed commentators of the time. Other types of evidence may be less reliable. For instance, biographies – even when written soon after the composer's lifetime – may include misremembered facts or the biographer may have let his own views influence the account.

The primary document, if it still exists, is often the composer's autograph score or an original recording of a jazz work – although composers sometimes revise their works for later performances and jazz musicians frequently devise new versions of previously recorded tracks. Sometimes an early published edition in which the composer has made corrections or other annotations (such as suggestions to a pupil for fingering or realising ornaments) may provide evidence. Further clues to how 18th-century music was performed may come from 'teach yourself' books that were published at the time – these were often weighty treatises that explain in detail the performing conventions of the day. The 18th-century composer, Quantz, wrote one on playing the flute, and Mozart's father, Leopold, wrote about playing the violin.

> An 'autograph score' is one in the composer's own handwriting.

**Facts**

A straight chronology of events, or list of dates when music was composed or first performed is one type of starting-point. Another might be geography – where were things happening? Whether a composer was Austrian or Italian, or whether a jazz band was playing in New Orleans or New York, might have made a difference to the style of the music. Who taught whom? Which performers are known to have worked together? Piecing together the trail that leads from one musician to another can cast light on our understanding of their music.

> When writing about dates, be careful not to confuse years with centuries. We live in the 21st century, but the years begin with 20, not 21. Similarly, 1780 is not in the 17th century but in the 18th century.

**Interpretation**

The evidence is analysed, hypotheses are explored, and judgements are made. The purpose is to help us understand why the music is as it is, how the composer would have expected it to sound and what it is 'about'. To answer these questions we need to apply different sorts of analytical skill.

In the examination you will be expected to be able to discuss what is known about the background context of the set works (particularly in Section C). You are not expected to do your own historical research but doing some additional reading will help you form a better picture in your mind. Some useful sources are listed in this guide.

You are expected to have studied the music itself very closely, first-hand, and to be able to discuss it using technical language. To do this successfully you will need to develop specialised analytic skills. These are discussed at the end of this section.

### Reception

'Reception' is a word used to describe how a work was regarded by audiences, critics and performers of the day as well as how perceptions of a work have changed over time. For instance, in the 19th century some writers referred to Mozart as 'divine' because his gifts were thought to be so great. Twentieth-century writers have looked more closely at the human being, the man behind the music, and found a much less 'divine' personality. This has not meant that his music has been valued less, but it does mean that our perception of what we hear and how we make sense of it may be different in the 21st century.

How the first performance of a piece of music is received depends on what the audience are expecting. If they are familiar with the style they may appreciate the work's inventiveness. Eighteenth-century audiences were used to hearing much new music, often specially composed for the occasion. If a work didn't sound up-to-the-minute they might complain that it seemed old-fashioned and stale, although if it was very innovative they could be shocked.

Study of the history of music in the mid-18th century was confined to a few enthusiasts. Awareness and appreciation of old music began to develop among musicians towards the end of the century and to spread more widely during the 19th century. By the 20th century it was common for orchestral concert programmes to give pride of place to the music of earlier composers, especially those who were by then recognised as great masters, while performances of new music became less common.

Conversely, jazz and popular music still depend on a constant stream of new music, although they too have their histories and there is a keen appreciation of landmark performances of the past.

### Transmission

How does music become known to an audience beyond those present at a first performance? Today, communications are immediate. Until the advent of photocopiers and computers with music-notation software, parts had to be copied by hand. Copying played an important role, too, in how students, composers and connoisseurs got to know new music. This was a slow process. But, by the end of the 18th century, the demand for music to perform at home had fuelled rapid growth in music publishing and composers in the next century were increasingly able to earn part of their living from sales of their music. But there was no copyright protection, so pirated editions and handwritten copies would quickly circulate if a first performance had been a success.

Connoisseurs (people with an expert understanding of an art) have been as important in music as in any other art form. For instance, many aristocrats were accomplished performers on instruments and some composed as well. They often had enough interest and wealth to commission new music, employ musicians and to accumulate libraries of music to perform and study.

Composers frequently dedicated music to them. Sponsorship is still important, although today funds are more likely to be channelled through charitable trusts, broadcasting companies and government agencies such as Arts Council England.

In the late 19th century, greater prosperity enabled more people to purchase pianos and sheet music to play at home, both coming down in price as a result of industrial manufacturing processes. This was followed, in the early 20th century, by radio and recording, which widened the audience for music further still. No longer was it necessary to journey to a large city to hear celebrated performers, or to pay high box-office prices – everyone could access the latest music cheaply and immediately. Recordings by different artists (or the same ones on different occasions) could easily be compared. Popular audiences became increasingly knowledgeable about the music they liked.

Reception and transmission are aspects of the study of the history of music that you may be asked about in Section C.

**Analytic techniques**

Some people find the term 'analysis' rather off-putting, but it simply means discovering how music works – an essential skill for any musician. It helps us to understand how styles and genres change over time, to trace the influence of one sort of music on another, to explain what appears to be a radical innovation – perhaps dispelling myths that portray it as one man's revolution overnight – and to categorise trends and identify common characteristics.

You will need to develop some analytic skills for the listening paper. In Section A you will be applying these to understanding an extract of *unfamiliar music*, listening and answering questions 'on the hoof'. In Section B you will already know the music well and will be expected, therefore, to be able to answer more probing analytic questions.

What is involved in analysis? First, you need a keen ear – you must be able to distinguish one instrument from another, one part from another, the treble, the bass, the keys, chords, cadences, repetition and variation, structure, and so on. Secondly, you need knowledge – to be able to identify specific techniques used in the music, such as sequences, pizzicato, imitation or pedal notes, and to give them their technical names. Finally, you need to be able to describe and explain how the music works in your own words.

Writing about music needs practice. There are many short exercises in this guide designed to help you build up the skills you need in order to be able to answer confidently in an examination. Work through them all slowly and don't skip any. Then you will be ready to get the greatest possible benefit from working through complete practice tests.

# Section A

This section of your exam is not just a test of aural perception: you will need to understand musical notation, know technical terms and be confident about identifying keys, chords and cadences. The recordings are accompanied by a skeleton score and you may be asked to write in a missing phrase of melody, notate part of a bass line, name chords or identify ornaments.

> A skeleton score gives an outline of the music, often on two staves, with enough detail for you to follow it as you listen, but it also has quite a lot of information missing. Bar numbers and CD timings are printed in the score to help you follow the recording.

Whichever extract you choose (1A on instrumental music from the period 1700–1830 or 1B on instrumental popular music from 1900 to the present day) it will usually consist of two or at most three short passages separated by short breaks. These will be labelled 'passage 1i', 'passage 1ii' and 'passage 1iii', and will all be from different sections of a single piece of music. Sometimes the second and third passages will be actual variations of a theme that was given in the first passage but, more often, they will simply use some of the same material as the first passage but in slightly different ways. As well as questions related to tonality and the expressive use of instrumental techniques, you might also be asked about the ways in which the later passages vary material from the first one.

Whichever extract you choose, its musical language will be tonal. The questions are a test of whether you can really hear the techniques you have been learning and using in your exercises for Section A of the composing unit.

**Tonality**

The scores will be straightforward, so that the notes are not too dense on the page or cluttered with too many other symbols. The examiners are more interested in what you can hear and whether you understand the tonal style than in setting you complicated writing tasks. But you do need to be able to read treble and bass clefs confidently, and to be able to notate pitches and common rhythmic patterns accurately, because you will be asked to notate short passages (on the score) in both clefs. Most importantly, you must be sure of your keys, not just recognising them from key signatures at the beginning of the score but hearing and identifying modulations that happen in the course of the extract. Making sure you can do this should be an important part of your preparation.

**Ornamentation**

Other aspects of the music that you might be asked to identify or explain include variation techniques, inessential notes and ornamentation. The sign for an ornament might be omitted and you could be asked to write it in the correct position on the score, or to give its name and describe what it does. The most common types of ornament are:

➤ A **trill** (*tr*) which consists of a rapid alternation between the printed note and the one above it. There are several examples in the Alla Hornpipe movement of Handel's *Water Music*. (The trill sign is also used to indicate a continuous roll on the timpani, e.g. in the first movement of Beethoven's Symphony No. 5, bars 249 and 251–252. However, instead of rapidly alternating between two notes, the timpanist must repeat the note printed.)

➤ A **turn** (∞) which starts on the note above the printed note, followed by the printed note itself, then the note below it, and finally the printed note once more. The closest example of a turn in the prescribed orchestral scores can be found in the first movement of Beethoven's Symphony No. 5. In bar 268, a turn is notated in full for the first oboe's brief cadenza; the four semiquavers that follow the minim D could have been replaced with a turn symbol.

➤ **Grace notes** are other short, ornamental notes. The **acciaccatura** (♪) is a note printed in small type with a slash through its tail; it is usually the note above the one it decorates. It must be played as quickly as possible, just before the beat. The appoggiatura (♪) is often the note above the one it ornaments, written without a slash; it leans onto the decorated note. (See examples in Mozart's Horn Concerto No. 4, e.g. bar 168 of the solo horn part.)

In the 18th century it was customary to start trills and turns on the note above the printed one, but there is no clear rule that covers every context. Modern interpretations may differ.

**Instruments and textures**

Throughout the AS course, techniques for combining instruments will keep coming under the spotlight and you should expect one or two questions about this aspect of the music in these extracts. As well as identifying instruments you should be prepared to recognise common performing techniques like glissando, pizzicato and the use of a mute.

If you are asked to *describe* the texture of a passage it is important to give as much detail as you can: explain if parts are in unison or doubled an octave above or below, identify the instruments and explain exactly who is doing what. If the texture is imitative, be specific – say which instrument begins, which comes in next, what the pitch interval between these two entries is, and so on.

Whether the passages in the extract you have chosen are described as variations or not, they will certainly be closely related to one another. You will be asked to identify the techniques that have been used to vary the original theme. This might be through change of key, tempo or harmony, different melodic decoration or changes in instrumentation and texture.

The use of variation techniques is not confined to the 18th century – if you choose extract 1B you will find that similar questions are asked. Almost all music includes variation of previously heard material and the techniques used are still important to composers today – could this include you, in your work for Section B of the composing unit? And, of course, variation is one of the most significant ingredients in jazz improvisation.

If you decide to answer questions on the popular music extract (1B) remember that it could come from before or after the period of the set jazz recordings that you will be studying (which come from the years 1920–1960). The style of the music may or may not be influenced by jazz. However, the types of question will be similar to those for extract 1A. There may be clear use of variation techniques but the extract may be from film music in which the original theme is altered significantly or reduced to one or two motifs for dramatic reasons.

## Variation techniques

For discussion and examples of variation techniques see *OCR AS Music Listening Tests, 4th edition* (Rhinegold Education, 2013).

## Exercise 19

The following extract is a skeleton score of the Lentement from Handel's *Water Music* Suite No. 2. Follow the score carefully while listening to a recording of it. Play it as many times as you need to in order to answer the questions that follow.

1. What chord is heard on the last beat of bar 4?

2. Name the cadence at bars $9^3$–10.

3. **On the score** complete the missing melody in bars 11–13.

4. a. Which pair of treble instruments play in bars 19–21?

   b. Name the interval between them.

5. a. Identify the key in bars 23–26.

   b. What is the relationship of this key to the tonic key of bars 1–18?

6. **On the score** complete the missing bass notes in bars $31^3$–$33^1$.

7. In what key does this extract end at bar 34?

8  a. Compare the music of bars 19–34 with that of bars 1–18. Name their similarities and differences (other than those asked in the questions above).

   b. Mention any other points that seem significant.

When you have answered all these questions check your answers against your own copy of the study score. Compare your answers with ours on page 68.

## Section B

**Extract 2**   There will be three tracks on your CD for this section of the paper. The first two of these will contain *different performances* of an extract from one of the three set orchestral works. They will be labelled 'Extract 2A' and 'Extract 2B' on the question paper. You may not bring copies of the scores into the examination room but you will be given a full score of the extract in the insert booklet (note that this score will not include CD timings).

The first few questions are usually about the **notation** of the score, such as the meaning of abbreviations or signs. You could be asked to transpose a clarinet or trumpet part into sounding pitch, or to write out on a treble or bass stave a viola phrase that is printed in the C clef. These are questions that you need to practise during the course – don't leave these skills until the night before the exam, especially since they are also likely to be needed when answering other types of questions.

There may well be one or two questions about **tonality** and tonal devices in this extract – a chord, a cadence, modulations and key relationships, sequences and pedal notes can all crop up. Recognising these in an orchestral score also needs practice.

You may be asked to describe the **texture** of the extract, to compare the passage with an earlier or later statement of the same theme (for which you will have to rely on your memory!), or to comment on how typical it is of this composer. Keep 'compare' questions in your mind as you study each score: notice when the woodwind are silent and when they play, whether they double the strings or have independent parts, what the difference is between the brass contributing a melody and simply filling out a chord, or which instruments sustain a dominant pedal.

You will be expected to be able to place the extract within the movement as a whole. To do this, you must know the outline **structure** of the movement and be able to recognise typical features of each section within it. You might be asked, for instance, whether an extract containing the second subject is from the exposition or the recapitulation (the clue usually lies in the key). Or, you might be asked to describe significant features of the music that comes before or after the actual extract.

The two recordings of the extract will have been chosen because they contrast in sound. Their interpretation of features such as tempo, dynamics, phrasing, ornamentation and articulation may differ. The orchestras themselves may not be made up the same way. One of the excerpts might have been recorded by a large orchestra of modern instruments while the other was recorded by a much smaller ensemble of 'period' instruments, with relatively few string players to each part. The latter type of performance might also be at a lower pitch than its modern equivalent, reflecting the fact that pitch in the period 1700–1830 was slightly lower than is usual today.

'Period' instruments are usually modern reconstructions that allow the performer to recreate the type of sound that might have been heard when early music was first performed.

Research into how music was performed in the past has also made it possible to use performing techniques that produce sounds more like the ones that the original composers would have expected to hear. This approach to performing music of the past is often referred to as **authentic** because it is said to be more faithful to the composer's intentions. Another view is that the music will sound different on modern instruments, but not necessarily worse, and that the composers of the past might well have welcomed the different sound.

You will not be asked to make a judgement about which of the performances is 'better', but you do need to understand some of the issues that will have influenced the two conductors in reaching their interpretative decisions.

Try to hear more than one type of recorded performance of each of your orchestral set works: all of them have been recorded many times during the last 50 years and historical research into styles of playing has influenced many of the more recent conductors.

Study the section on 'The score' in the next chapter (page 70) and work through all the exercises in it. This will give you the information and basic techniques needed to get started. Then tackle one of the three orchestral set works. Listen with the score to more than one recording if at all possible. The more often you do this, the more easily you will be able to make musical sense of the score for yourself. Then, when the *sound* of each piece has begun to take root inside your head, study the relevant section in the chapter on the orchestral set works. Use your reading to inform your hearing – not the other way round. Don't treat the recordings as 'add-ons' to the information you read.

**Extract 3**

The third extract will be from one of the three set jazz recordings (see the list on page 69). There will be no score, so the questions will usually be about things that you can hear clearly on the recording.

There will be questions about the instruments and how they are used. You may be asked to describe the texture of a particular passage. Your answer should show that you understand the role of each instrument, whether frontline or rhythm section, and you should be prepared to describe particular features of the music that each plays, including any special effects such as glissando or the use of a mute. You should also be able to recognise compositional devices used in the music, such as call-and-response, secondary rag or collective improvisation.

You may be asked to relate the extract to an earlier part of the piece that is not heard on the recording. You will need to remember the outline structure of the whole work and know it well enough to recognise exactly where the recorded extract comes in it. You will be expected to be able to describe the music that follows the extract, so you will need to be sure of the order of solo and chorus sections and be able to describe their main features.

You should know the names of the main performers in the band, particularly those who make a significant contribution to the music, including soloists and the rhythm section.

## Section C

The last question in the examination will be an essay on one or more of the set works. Further details and practice questions are given in the Section C questions chapter of this book, starting on page 145.

### Answers for Exercise 19

1. Second inversion tonic chord / Ic.

2. Imperfect. The chord in bars 10–11 is the dominant / V.

3. Check against your own copy of the score.

4. a. Oboes.

   b. 3rd (a mixture of minor and major 3rds).

5. a. B minor (the chord in bar 26 is its dominant, F♯ major)

   b. Relative minor (of the tonic key, D major).

6. Check against your own copy of the score. (Notice how the harmonic rhythm quickens here in the approach to the perfect cadence.)

7. E minor.

8  a. Similarities: rhythm (the dotted rhythm in the melody and regular minim/crotchet rhythm in the bass); melodic shape (almost the entire piece grows out of the pattern set out in the opening bars – illustrate your answer by referring to specific bars). Differences: some phrases that use an identical melody are harmonised differently (e.g. bars 1–5 and 19–23); one of them, bars 27–31, extends its phrase by additional repetition.

8  b. The second section of this movement is arranged differently to the first section: it omits horns and trumpets (because of the modulations). In bars 21–23 the strings alone echo the oboes and bassoon phrase of bars 19–21, using the same, but thicker, harmonies (violas provide an additional middle line).

# Set works

For Sections B and C of the paper you have to study six set works (described by OCR as the 'prescribed repertoire') – three orchestral scores from the 18th and early 19th centuries, plus three jazz recordings, from the period 1920–1960.

It is very important to check carefully that you are studying the right combination of pieces for the year in which you are going to take the exam:

## Orchestral scores

| June 2014 to June 2015 | 1. Handel: *Water Music* Suite No.2 in D, HWV349 (Allegro, Alla Hornpipe, Menuet, Lentement and Bourrée) |
| | 2. Mozart: Concerto No. 4 in E♭ for Horn and Orchestra, K.495 (third movement) |
| | 3. Beethoven: Symphony No. 5 in C minor, Op. 67 (first movement) |

## Jazz recordings

| June 2014 | 1. Louis Armstrong and His Hot Five: *Hotter Than That* (1927) from *Louis Armstrong 25 Greatest Hot Fives & Hot Sevens*, Living Era AJA 5171 (ASIN B000001H15) |
| | 2. Duke Ellington: *Koko* (1940) from *Cotton Tail: Classic Recordings, Vol. 7* (1940), Naxos Jazz Legends 8.120738 (ASIN B00030B9AC) |
| | 3. Miles Davis: *Boplicity* from *Birth of the Cool* (1949), on *Birth of the Cool, Rudy Van Gelder (RVG) Edition* (original recording remastered), Capitol Jazz/Blue Note Records 7 24353 0117 2 7 (ASIN B00005614M). [The original recording can also be found on the CD specified for use with the previous OCR Music specification: Capitol Jazz 0777 7 92862 2 5 (ASIN B000005HF9).] |
| June 2015 to June 2016 | 1. New Orleans Rhythm Kings: *Tin Roof Blues* (13 March 1923 – Take 2) from *New Orleans Rhythm Kings 1922–1925: The Complete Set*, Retrieval Records |
| | 2. Dizzy Gillespie & His Orchestra: *Manteca* (30 December 1947) from *Dizzy Gillespie: The Ultimate Collection* OR *Dizzy Gillespie: The Complete RCA Victor Recordings*, RCA / Bluebird Records 07863665282 (1995) |
| | 3. Miles Davis Quintet: *'Round About Midnight (Legacy Edition – Remastered)* (10 September 1956) from Columbia Legacy / Sony Jazz 5199572 (2005) [NB The prescribed recording is the opening track on disk 1, <u>not</u> the Newport Jazz Festival performance of 1955 recorded on disk 2] |

Note that any edition and any recording of the orchestral scores may be used but you *must* make sure that the jazz recordings you study are *exactly* the ones listed above.

# Orchestral scores

You will be provided with a copy of the music for Extract 2 in the examination paper. The extract will be from one of your three prescribed orchestral scores.

Bars are usually numbered from the first complete bar onwards and superscript numerals are used for beats, so bar $8^1$ means the first beat of bar 8.

It won't look exactly the same as the copy that you have been using during your course but it will use the standard conventions and format found in most modern editions. Bars will be numbered from the beginning of the extract, so are unlikely to coincide with the bar numbering of the complete piece. To be able to answer the questions about the work sucessfully you will need to understand some of the conventions for notating and interpreting scores.

## The score

**Editions**

Editions may vary: the Bärenreiter edition of the last movement of Mozart's Horn Concerto No. 4, K. 495 agrees with the Eulenburg score until bar 109. Because it repeats four bars the Bärenreiter numbering after this point always adds four bars. Both sets of numbering are given in this book, Eulenburg first, then Bärenreiter in square brackets.

Most scores you use in class will probably be miniature, pocket or study editions. Modern conductors use much larger full scores that allow them to read the notes more easily while standing. Scores of orchestral music were rarely published in printed form before the 19th century. In the early and mid-18th century, performances were usually directed from the harpsichord, often by the composer himself. If the composer was also the soloist in a concerto the solo part could be incomplete, the remainder being improvised on the night. The performance was often a very last-minute affair – it is no exaggeration to say that the ink on the page was sometimes still wet! The score was the master document from which a copyist rushed to prepare individual parts for the performers.

During the 19th century a public market for printed scores developed, sometimes copied and published without the composer's permission. The reputation of a work could spread widely, far beyond the big cities where there were opportunities to hear it performed, and people began to want to get to know fashionable pieces, not just hear them once only. Sometimes the first opportunity to hear a work would be in an arrangement for piano given by a touring virtuoso. Playing piano-duet versions of symphonies and overtures at home was a popular way of getting to know the classics of the orchestral repertoire in the late 19th and early 20th centuries.

With the advent of recording and broadcasting, and the growth of international tours, opportunities to hear and rehear orchestral music in different interpretations increased, and with these came a demand for cheaply-printed, pocket-sized scores for study purposes. Audiences began to be knowledgeable and critical about how music was performed. They could compare different approaches of conductors and performers, who often consciously tried to impose their own personal stamp on the music.

In the second half of the 20th century performers and scholars everywhere became concerned to ensure that the scores used in the preparation of performances reproduced what the composer had originally written more reliably – in other words, that they were authentic. Editors sought out manuscripts and the earliest printed editions, comparing them and trying to resolve problems or discrepancies between them in the light of what they knew about the conventions of the composer's time – in other words, performance practice. The result of such careful scholarship is often the publication of what is called an Urtext (original text) edition, which usually includes a detailed account of how the different sources have been used. Critical scores have also become common; these give a great deal more background information about the genesis of the music, and if the composer left any rough drafts of the work these might be included as well.

OCR does not require you to use any particular edition or recording of the orchestral scores. Depending on what your school or college has in its collection you may be working from a recent Urtext or from a much earlier, edited score. You should be aware that there might be differences, and some of the detail in the extract used in the exam might not be identical to the score you have been using. However, it is not necessary to study more than one edition of any of the orchestral set works.

## Notation

Most modern scores use a standard format that may be different from the original layout used by the composer. Instruments are grouped into sections – woodwind at the top, followed by horns, then any other brass and percussion, then strings at the bottom. Music for woodwind and string instruments is printed in order of pitch – highest at the top, lowest at the bottom. If there is a solo instrument (as in the Mozart Horn Concerto), its part is usually shown immediately above the strings.

Instrument names are often in Italian, but most are easily recognisable (such as *flauto*, a flute). Oboes and bassoons (*fagotti*) were the original staples of the woodwind section, with the flute making an occasional appearance. Clarinets were added towards the end of the 18th century. By about 1800 the woodwind were usually scored in pairs (two flutes, two oboes, two clarinets and two bassoons) – a layout known as **double woodwind**.

Horns (*corni*) were also usually used in pairs in the 18th century and are always placed above the trumpets in the score, reflecting the fact that they are often used to blend with the woodwind. In some scores trumpets (*trombe*) may be named as *clarino* – be careful not to confuse these with clarinets.

Throughout the 18th century, the percussion normally consisted of just a pair of timpani played by one person. The notes to which they are to be tuned are given at the beginning of the score and are usually the tonic and dominant of the main key (C and G in the Beethoven movement).

Double basses (*contrabassi*) usually play the same notes as the cellos, but sound an octave lower. In scores of 18th century music there is often only one stave for both instruments, labelled 'Basso'. However, in Beethoven's Symphony No. 5, these two instruments are usually given separate lines to specify certain effects. For example, in bars 1–5 in the first movement, the double bass part is notated an octave higher to ensure that both sets of instruments actually play in unison. In bar 7, the double basses drop out altogether. In the passage at bars 331–346, the cellos and double basses are separated to allow the basses to maintain the rhythmic figure in the background, against the crotchets of the melodic line.

To get a fuller texture, the composer may divide a string part between the available players. Many chords can be played on string instruments (known as 'double-stopping'), such as the first and second violin chords in bars 45–48 in the last movement of Mozart's Horn Concerto No. 4. The notes can be played by drawing the bow quickly across the lower strings. However, in bars 99–105, it is not possible to play these combinations of notes so the violas have to divide and share the two lines between them (doubling first and second violins an octave lower).

If a pair of wind instruments has only a single line of music then both are expected to play – unless it is marked *solo* to show that only the first instrument is required. The direction *a 2* will appear if they are then to resume playing in unison. The figures 1. and 2., or the use of upward or downward stems on the notes, may also indicate which instrument is to play.

Scores did not specify how many string players were required – it depended on factors such as the number of wind parts, size of the venue, what could be afforded and availability of players. The author of the *Musikalisches Lexicon* (musical dictionary), published in 1802, recommended six first violins, six second violins, four violas, four cellos and three double basses for symphonies – 23 string players in total – although both smaller and larger string sections than this were used during the 18th century, depending on circumstances. In comparison, a modern symphony orchestra is likely to have around 60 string players.

You need to develop an ability to 'hear' internally the sounds that the score suggests – not just the melodic lines, but the rhythms and harmonies, the timbres of individual instruments, and the effects of combining them in different types of texture. This will become easier after studying and repeatedly listening to the music.

**Clefs**

As well as treble and bass clefs you will need to learn to find your way around the C clef (𝄡). This is used for several mid-range instruments which would otherwise need a lot of leger lines if notated using either treble or bass clefs.

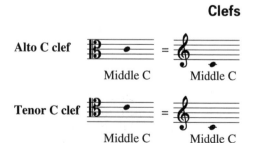

Alto C clef — Middle C = Middle C

Tenor C clef — Middle C = Middle C

Wherever the C clef is placed on a stave, the stave-line through its centre fixes the position of middle C, as shown left. The alto C clef straddles the middle line of the stave and is used for viola parts, while the tenor C clef is one line higher and is used for notes in the upper registers of the bassoon, trombone and cello.

## Exercise 20

If you are asked to rewrite a C-clef passage into either the treble or bass clef, use middle C as a reference point and check every few notes that you haven't slipped in pitch as you go. When you are asked to write out a part in a different clef always remember to put the correct key signature at the beginning of the stave.

1. Write out the following viola part using the treble clef:

Handel: *Water Music* HWV 349/12, Alla hornpipe

2. Write out the following bassoon parts twice: i) using the treble clef and ii) using the bass clef:

Beethoven Symphony No. 5, movement 1

Notice how notating the parts in the C clef has avoided the use of any leger lines.

If you look at the lists of instruments at the beginning of your Mozart and Beethoven scores you will almost certainly see the letter Eb beside the names of the horns (*corni*), and notice that these parts normally have no key signatures. In the 18th and early 19th centuries, the number and range of notes that a single instrument could play was very limited – horns (and trumpets) usually had to be pitched in the tonic key of the piece. The composer always wrote the part as though it was in C major: this was an indication to the player of where the notes lay on the instrument, not of their actual pitch. For example, in bars 15–16 of the last movement of Mozart's Horn Concerto No. 4, the parts for the two orchestral horns are notated as:

However, the instruments actually sound (i.e. at concert pitch) as follows:

Horns in D sound a minor 7th lower than the notes written for them:

7                Handel *Water Music* HWV 349/14, Lentement

Some modern scores, such as Bärenreiter's 2008 edition for Handel's *Water Music*, print horn parts at sounding pitch with a key signature. The Eulenberg score prints the trumpet parts this way as well, but not the parts for horns in D.

When the score shows the note C for a transposing instrument, the sound (concert pitch) that the instrument will produce will be the note given beside its name in the list at the beginning of the score.

Modern horns (almost always pitched in F) and trumpets (most often in B♭) are still notated as though they were in C major, but the addition of valves has made them more versatile. Performers can now modulate freely and play chromatic notes.

Clarinets are also notated as transposing instruments. Their pitch is most often either B♭ or A, depending on which suits the key of the piece better. If you look at the opening of your Beethoven score you will see that, confusingly, clarinets have a key signature of one flat (D minor). This is because the B♭ clarinet sounds a tone lower than is written – therefore, its key signature has to be a tone higher than the key of the piece (which is C minor).

> If your score of the Beethoven Symphony is that of a German publisher (e.g. Eulenburg), then the letter that will indicate B♭ clarinets will be 'B'.

Learning to identify quickly what the concert-pitch notes are that horns, trumpets and clarinets are playing is a skill which you must practise. You will almost certainly be given a few bars of music for one of these transposing instruments in the examination question paper and be asked to write them out at concert pitch. If you can become confident at doing this then you will also find it easier to identify chords and keys accurately in your scores.

## Exercise 21

1. Write out at concert pitch the following bars for clarinets. (Remember to put the appropriate key signature.)

Beethoven Symphony No. 5, movement 1

2. Look at the score of the third movement from Mozart's Horn Concerto No. 4, bars 136–151 [140–155].

   a. Write out at concert pitch the solo horn part from the last quaver of bar 136 [140] to the first crotchet of bar 151 [155]. (Remember that the horn is pitched in E♭.)

   b. In what key does this passage begin?

   c. Using Roman numerals identify the three chords in bars 139–140 [143–144].

   d. What note do the violas play throughout bars 141–145 [145–149]?

   e. How does the harmony change in bars 141–144 [145–148]?

   f. Where in the passage do the violas play in unison with the cellos?

   g. What does the instruction 'a2' mean in the oboe and orchestral horn parts at bar 151 [155]?

## Interpretation

Getting the notes right is the first priority for an orchestra but there's more to a good performance than just that. How the notes are played is important. Most composers will have given some guidance about this in their scores using performance directions. These musical terms are often written in Italian – you will need to learn the meanings of the words and symbols covered in the following sections.

**Tempo**    *Allegro* – the word used by all three composers at the start of your orchestral scores. Originally, it suggested that the music should be performed in a 'lively' way, but it gradually came to be understood as indicating a fast tempo. Beethoven adds '*con brio*' to ensure the liveliness.

---

### Exercise 22

Listen to recordings of the opening eight bars of each of your three prescribed orchestral scores. Compare the speed/tempo of their beats. In both the Handel and Beethoven movements the beats are crotchets; in the Mozart movement the beats are dotted crotchets. Which of the three works sounds the slowest? (If you have a metronome available, check your answer.)

---

It is rare to hear a performance of any long movement from the 18th or early 19th century in which the tempo is exactly the same all the way through. Particularly in concertos, there will be moments when the soloist may want to use **rubato**, which allows freedom to be more expressive by varying the tempo. Furthermore, conductors vary considerably in the way they bring movements to an end: some slow down a little; some a great deal; some hardly at all. Practise identifying fluctuations in tempo when you listen to different interpretations of your set works so that you can be quick to spot them in the recordings you are given to compare in the examination.

---

### Exercise 23

1. Compare the tempos of at least two recordings of the second and third movements of Handel's *Water Music* (Suite No. 2, Alla Hornpipe and Menuet).

    a. Does either performance vary in tempo, for example using a *rallentando* anywhere (i.e. slow down)? If so, mark it on your score.

    b. Is there a difference between the two recordings when sections are repeated?

---

**Articulation**

There are many different (articulation) signs that composers use to tell performers how to play each note: whether to detach it (*staccato*), accent it (*marcato*), hold it firmly (*tenuto*), or run it smoothly into the next note (*legato*). How performers understand these signs changes over time, and their meaning might vary slightly from composer to composer. When you compare recordings of your orchestral set works you may notice that one conductor consistently interprets staccato markings as a very slight shortening of notes, while another might cut them much shorter. Get into the habit of listening out for these very subtle differences in interpretation.

Some articulation signs mean specific things to different instrumentalists: for example, the way slurs are used in a melody tells wind players how to tongue it; for string players it suggests how the melody should be bowed. There are some other signs that apply only to string instruments:

➢ **Pizzicato** (usually abbreviated to 'pizz.') tells players when to pluck the strings

➢ **Arco** tells them when to resume using the bow

> ➤ **Tremolo** is notated by strokes through the beam of the note to indicate rapid repetitions: the number of strokes determines the speed of the repetitions.

The two strokes through the crotchet and minims in the music example to the left indicate that performers are to repeat the note to its full value using semiquavers. It may also be used in this way for timpani parts, but a long roll is more often written as *tr* (trill).

**Dynamics**

In the 18th century composers wrote very few dynamic markings into their scores, as they expected performers to be thoroughly familiar with the conventions of the day. In a solo concerto the orchestral *tutti* (sections where all parts play the *ritornello*) would sound as loud whether they were marked *f* (*forte*) or not. The solo episodes were usually more lightly scored, and the orchestral parts might have indications for *p* (*piano*).

By the early 19th century, however, Beethoven was notating dynamic markings very carefully, often demanding extremes of loud and soft.

## Exercise 24

1. Following your score, listen to a recording of bars 158–252 from the first movement of Beethoven's Symphony No. 5.

   a. Where is the softest passage? Give precise bar numbers to show where it begins and ends.

   b. How does the scoring (instrumentation/orchestration) help to make bars 248–252 the loudest in the extract?

Although there are machines that can measure noise levels accurately in decibels, judging the changes in dynamic levels throughout a piece of music is very subjective. When you listen to your set works try to notice how different conductors handle dynamics: perhaps one interpretation will seem to work better than another? Ask yourself whether the contrasts are too sudden, too extreme, and whether there is enough contrast, or too much?

Orchestral scores contain a great deal of information and to begin following scores you may want to concentrate on keeping up with the music, probably by following the melody, whichever part it is in. As you become more familiar with the sound, and how it relates to the layout, practise trying to hear how different instruments perform different roles in the texture.

Get into the habit of noticing the effect of different timbres, how various combinations of instruments are used, and how a composer can create a crescendo by piling on the instruments rather than just increasing the dynamic levels.

As you listen, sometimes focus on details, sometimes listen to the whole: your eye on the score can identify techniques and effects which your ear may only be dimly aware of at first.

From time to time you may notice something that strikes you as an effective technique or combination of instruments that might be adapted for use in your own compositions. You could begin by experimenting with the variety of expressive sounds that can be obtained by different sorts of doubling.

## The Composers

The three orchestral works you will be studying for Section B were all composed within the space of a hundred years:

➢ Handel's *Water Music Suite* No. 2 in 1717

➢ Mozart's Horn Concerto No. 4 in 1786

➢ Beethoven's Symphony No. 5 in 1808.

It is important to get their chronology straight in your mind. You may also find it helpful to understand something about the nationalities of the three composers and why they chose to work in the cities they did.

All three were native speakers of German, but Germany was not yet the single, unified nation that we know today. Spread across Central and Eastern Europe there were many small states, a great number of which were part of a large empire. The Imperial Palace and its administrative centre were in the Austrian city of Vienna. Vienna was, therefore, not only a court to which ambassadors from all over the world were attached, but one made up of many princes, dukes, and lesser nobility, who were also rulers in their own parts of the Empire. Handel's employer, the king of Hanover, was known as the 'Elector' of Hanover because he was one of those who held the right to elect the Emperor.

# Handel (1685 – 1759)

Handel was born in Halle in Saxony (where Hanover was the capital city). As a young man he travelled widely, including to Italy, learning the ins-and-outs of composing Italian opera. After a brief time in Hanover, at the Elector's court, he moved to London where he knew there were good opportunities opening up for a composer of Italian opera. The English aristocracy was developing a strong appetite for this newly-imported genre (sung in Italian by mainly Italian singers). His first opera, *Rinaldo* (1711), was a great success and Handel was soon very much in favour at court: Queen Anne awarded him a pension of £200 a year. When she died in 1714, by a strange quirk of English law, it was the Elector of Hanover who succeeded her as King George I. Handel stayed in London, eventually becoming a British citizen.

By the time Handel died in 1759 he was almost revered as a native English composer. During his lifetime musical fashions had changed: Italian opera had been overtaken by a middle-class taste for oratorios (dramatic music on biblical themes, sung in English, composed in the Italian style but not acted on stage). Handel was the leading composer of this genre – the best-known being his *Messiah* (1742).

Handel was one of the principal benefactors of the Foundling Hospital in London, giving it the proceeds of several performances of *Messiah*. The Foundling Museum, in Brunswick Square, offers an interesting introduction to the composer and his times.

## Mozart (1756 – 1791)

In 1790, Mozart's great friend and mentor Haydn had been invited to London to compose symphonies for a series of concerts. On a return visit, Haydn was so impressed by a performance of *Messiah*, with a huge choir and orchestra in Westminster Abbey, that he then composed an oratorio, *The Creation* (1798).

Mozart's father brought his son to London in 1764, five years after Handel's death. The child was eight years old, a musical prodigy being put on show in a gruelling concert tour which had taken him and his sister to the most important cities across Europe. Not only was the young Mozart already an accomplished performer and improviser, he was also a precocious composer. In London, the fashionable composers were now Johann Christian Bach (youngest son of the 'great' J.S. Bach) and Carl Friedrich Abel (both also of German origin). Mozart learned a great deal from them. He would undoubtedly have encountered the music of Handel. Much later, Mozart was to share the enthusiasm and respect for Handel's oratorios which fired an inner circle of Viennese musicians and music-lovers in the 1780s, and copies of the dead composer's music began to circulate there. In 1789 Mozart paid his own tribute in a 'modernising' re-orchestration and performance of *Messiah*.

As Vienna grew into a thriving business city during the 18th century, it also became an influential cultural centre, a magnet which attracted musicians from all over the world. Many stayed, but there was also a great deal of coming-and-going, in spite of what would seem to us now as formidable travelling difficulties. Other fashionable cities, such as Paris and London, and many in Italy (Venice, Naples, Rome, Milan) were also on the concert circuit. Although there were sometimes strong regional differences in the sort of music that local audiences enjoyed, there were also styles that became popular internationally. One of the most successful of these was Italian opera (to which Mozart was also drawn), and another was the style of purely instrumental music that developed rapidly in late-18th century Vienna.

Mozart had been born and grew up in Salzburg (now a part of modern Austria). At that time Salzburg was an independent state ruled by an Archbishop, by whom Mozart was briefly employed when he was a young man. However, Mozart found the atmosphere provincial and stifling, and hated the working conditions, so, like Handel, he moved on, but in his case to Vienna.

## Beethoven (1770 – 1827)

Beethoven arrived in Vienna, from his home town of Bonn, in 1790. He too was hoping to make his reputation (and earn a living) as a pianist and composer. He had a few disappointing lessons in composing from Haydn, but had probably already learned all that he could from close study of the older man's music. He admired the music of Mozart, whose death the following year was deeply mourned.

## Context

None of these composers worked in a vacuum. They kept a close ear on their competitors' music, knew what would attract a fee-paying audience, and what would sell well when published. The concert-going public had a thirst for novelty but was less quick to accept complete originality – they liked music to be *new*, but still within the bounds of a familiar style.

In the early 19th century Beethoven was the first to overcome this ambivalence, but he too sometimes pushed these boundaries beyond the limits of ready acceptability. His listeners had to work hard to get to grips with his music. He was more fortunate than Mozart in securing the support of a group of influential aristocrats who guaranteed him a pension.

The three pieces you are to study show the three composers all working in different ways. Handel's *Water Music* was a commission for a royal occasion. Throughout his life Handel re-worked bits and pieces of earlier music, sometimes his own, sometimes that of other composers. It is no surprise that many of the tunes in the *Water Music* had first been heard in operas (George I was a keen opera-goer).

Financially, Mozart led a hand-to-mouth existence, struggling to survive independently. When he did have a commission, or a concert was imminent, his ability to compose quickly, under pressure to meet the deadline, is well known, as was the tendency for the music to be almost completely formed in his head before he put pen to paper. The horn concertos, however, were composed for pleasure, as a favour to a good friend, and their composition was spread over a longer period of time.

> On hearing a new Mozart opera in 1781, the Emperor Joseph II complained that the work contained 'too many notes'; Mozart replied that there were just as many as were necessary.

Once Beethoven was established in Vienna he composed bigger and grander pieces – the ideas taking shape over long periods of time in his sketch books, which often show the music developing from quite small germs. His manuscripts are full of crossings-out and second thoughts. He was his own severest critic, composing to satisfy himself. He was also a shrewd businessman. By the beginning of the 19th century composers could earn a significant income from publishing. He had, in fact promised the score of the Fifth Symphony to a music-loving aristocrat, and even been paid an advance on it, but in the end he dedicated it to his regular patrons and lost no time in getting it published.

Although Beethoven never came to England, all his new music was devoured by his fans as soon as it arrived, and it was an English musical society, the Philharmonic Society of London, that commissioned his last symphony (No. 9). He was also a keen student of Handel's music, and was seen by visitors shortly before his death in 1827 sitting up in bed immersed in the latest volume, which was being published in a new edition.

## Handel: *Water Music* Suite No. 2 in D, HWV 349

### First Performance

George I's position as the new king of England was a delicate one: he was a foreigner and a very remote relation of the late queen. He had succeeded to the British crown only because he happened to be a Protestant. A rather private man, he disliked ceremonial appearances but, when he was persuaded by an adviser at court that he needed to raise his public profile, he agreed to a concert on the Thames. A great deal is known about the costs of the event, but it is not known what Handel made from the evening, if anything, other than increased favour at court.

The occasion is well-documented: it caused such a stir that there were numerous accounts, including one in the daily newspaper and another in a letter from a diplomat reporting home to the court in Berlin: 'The music had been composed expressly for the occasion by the famous Handel, a native of Halle, the king's principal composer. The king so liked the music that he had it played three times, even though each playing lasted an hour, twice before and once after, supper.'

The large procession of boats set off from Whitehall about 8 o'clock on the evening of 17th July, 1717. They went with the flow of the tide as much as possible, using oars only as necessary. The king was in the most splendid of them all, with a small group of his favourites, seated in the luxuriously decorated, comfortable cabin; the oarsmen, seated in pairs, filled the rest of the barge. The rest of the court were in numerous other boats. The musicians were in a large barge, big enough for 50 of them (mostly standing) and perhaps as many as 18 oarsmen.

The 2012 Royal Jubilee Pageant was the most recent in a long tradition of royal processions by boat on the Thames.

A typical 18th-century royal barge, similar to the one used on the occasion of Handel's *Water Music*. This one can be seen in the National Maritime Museum in Greenwich.

Trumpets, when used ceremonially, usually went hand-in-hand with timpani, but timpani were not included this time, perhaps because there wasn't room for them. Perhaps for the same reason, the usual practice of having a harpsichordist improvise, completing the harmonies from a bass line with figures (known as a **continuo** part), was not followed. Sometimes other chordal instruments, such as lutes, were used to do this instead of a harpsichord, but their sound would have been almost inaudible across the water. Handel composed all the music to be self-sufficient: the chords were so complete, in well-balanced textures that could be heard clearly, that harpsichord filling was not necessary. Handel is said to have conducted, but quite how is not certain.

It is quite common for orchestras today to decide to add continuo instruments.

Most of the musicians would already have been known to the composer, many of them playing regularly in the theatre. Although always rather special occasions, water parties were not uncommon and they were often accompanied by music. Some of the performers would have participated in this sort of event before, but on a smaller scale: it is possible that some of the music played that night had been used by Handel previously on a similar occasion.

However, the horn players seem to have been brought in specially, probably from Bohemia (now part of the Czech Republic) or Germany. The instrument's popularity had developed rapidly after Count von Spork, a Bohemian aristocrat on a visit to France in the 1680s, had taken such a liking to the sound of the horns he heard in Paris that he arranged for two of his men to learn to play the instrument. On his return home he encouraged its use and, by the beginning of the 18th century, the 'French' horn was to be heard in many European cities, particularly German-speaking ones. Handel's prominent use of the instrument in London was something of a novelty.

The title, *Water Music*, is a shorthand label for the 22 pieces that were played that night. The only thing that connects them to water is the occasion: it is not descriptive music.

The music had to serve two purposes: to be regal and opulent, reflecting the majesty and position of the king – hence the inclusion of trumpets – and it had to please George I personally. He was a keen and discerning music-lover. The music has an international flavour: composing in a wide variety of styles, particularly French and Italian, Handel played down the German-ness of himself and the king, and showed that he had also learned to appreciate English musical traditions. Although English music had its own distinctive styles and traditions there had long been keen interest in the latest music from abroad.

> One of Handel's German contemporaries, Telemann, did compose a set of pieces that were descriptive: *Wassermusik* was written for an official celebration of the importance of the sea in Hamburg in 1723.

> At Elizabeth I's court in the late-16th century, Italian music was highly fashionable for a while; then, when Charles II returned from exile in France in 1660, he had developed an appetite for French music, a style that English composers again learned to absorb.

## Scores

It is unlikely that Handel 'conducted' from the sort of orchestral score that modern conductors use. None of the music was printed until later in the 18th century. After Handel's death, a succession of editors has tried to work out in what order the pieces were played that night. Reliable accounts say that the king liked the music so much he commanded it to be played three times and some of the individual pieces themselves have headings that say 'To be played three times'. It has gradually become customary to group the 22 pieces, which survive in different manuscript copies, into three suites, each grouped roughly by instrumentation and keys.

> A suite is a common musical term for a collection of dance pieces in the 18th century.

The OCR specification leaves you free to choose which modern edition you use. It lists the pieces in the order in which they were most commonly performed throughout the 20th century: Suite No. 2, HWV 349 (Allegro, Alla Hornpipe, Menuet, Lentement and Bourrée). This is the order used in the score published by Eulenburg, which is available for free download on the internet. This is quite adequate for you to use in preparation for the examination.

Bärenreiter's 2008 score is based on the most up-to-date scholarship, following the finding of a much earlier copy than had previously been known of all the music that made up the *Water Music*. This edition prints them in what is now believed to have been the original order of performance, which differs in significant ways from the three suites with which most musicians are familiar. When using this score, you

HWV stands for Händel Werke Verzeichnis, the catalogue of the composer's complete works.

There is also a very old score available as a download: a Dover reprint of a 19th-century edition, but it is not recommended.

will need to identify the precise pieces prescribed by OCR by checking their individual HWV numbers. In the following commentaries the pieces are discussed in the order in which they appear in the Eulenburg score, but the HWV numbers are also given, for those using the Bärenreiter edition.

The instruments used in what is known as the Second Suite in D do not include flutes or recorders, although they were used in other pieces of the *Water Music*. Here, besides parts for 1st and 2nd violins (and briefly for 3rd violins), violas, and cellos and basses (on the same stave), there are wind parts for two oboes and a bassoon, two trumpets and two horns. But, in the open air, on a river with boats separated from one another, there would have been an obvious need to strengthen the sound of the weaker instruments: it is believed that the total band of 50 musicians that night included many more than just two oboists and one bassoonist.

An unusual aspect of the Eulenburg score is that it uses the old English tradition of notating trumpet parts exactly as they sounded, even with the appropriate key signature. This was a practice that Handel usually followed. The horns, however, although pitched in D (like the trumpets), are given as transposing instruments in C. In the Bärenreiter score, however, the music for both pairs of instruments is written in D, with key signature. Beware! When you compare the trumpet and horn parts, they often appear to be playing exactly the same music, either simultaneously (as in the Trumpet Minuet, HWV 349/13) or one after another (as in the Allegro, HWV 349/11). Listen carefully and you will hear that the horns actually play an octave lower than the trumpets, i.e. for parts notated 'Horns in D', the transposition is a minor 9th down (not a major 2nd up, as it would be for trumpets in D). This, of course, intensifies the interest of their contrasting sonorities when they imitate one another, and increases the solidity of the harmony when they play together. This made them perfectly suited to an outdoor performance.

Handel shows off the contrast of pitch and timbres between trumpets and horn in the first piece you have to study, the Allegro.

## HWV 349/11: Allegro

Handel uses his orchestra as two distinct groups that play alternately:

➢ The upper group always consists of 1st and 2nd violins and violas, oboes and trumpets.

➢ The lower group consists of horns, cellos with basses, and bassoon(s).

What appears to be quite a long movement in fact consists of about 20 bars of music, always stated first by the upper (trumpet) group, then repeated by the lower (horn) group, but from bar 37 the two groups join together for a tutti section. This pattern is set up right at the start of the piece.

**Bars 1–5**   In a rousing fanfare, the trumpets stride up the tonic chord followed by a melodic flourish of semiquavers on the dominant; the strings and oboes hurtle in unison down a rapid D major scale.

Copied an octave down by the lower group, accompanied by bass instruments only (bassoons, cellos/basses), the horns stand out well, even though much less bright than trumpets. A short, 2-bar exchange in crotchets follows, almost as though horns are determined to dog the trumpets' footsteps.

In a composition designed to feature horns and trumpets so prominently, their restricted melodic function limits the variety of harmonies that can be used. Handel makes the most of the simple tonic/dominant chords, which form the basis of most of the musical material, by clothing them in a succession of varying rhythmic figures. The pattern of alternating phrases continues throughout the piece.

**Bars 5–9**

The two groups combine in a grand tutti that is repeated: the dotted crotchets of bars 38-40 are filled out with insistent quavers (e.g. bar 41) that drive the music towards its cadence (bars 44–45). The cadence is repeated, spaced out with rests, to bring the movement to its natural close at bar 47. Handel then adds three bars in quite a different tempo and mood (Adagio), which suggest a link, either to a repeat, or to the next movement. Links between movements were quite common at this time but the purpose of these bars is not clear. They lead to an imperfect cadence in the relative minor key of B minor, which leaves the end of the movement unresolved. The slow speed and rests between the chords offer an opportunity for a soloist to improvise. You may hear such an improvisation in different recordings, probably by the leader of the 1st violins.

**Bars 37²–50**

> This type of imperfect cadence in a minor key was a common feature at the time of writing. It is known as a Phrygian cadence, a term that relates it to an earlier modal system.

## HWV 349/12: Alla hornpipe

The hornpipe was a lively English country dance, typically in $\frac{3}{2}$ time and often heavily syncopated, as is this movement.

This section is complete in itself. Handel again varies the scoring: although the opening also sounds rather fanfare-like, in fact both trumpets and horns are silent – it is the strings and woodwind that open. Trumpets wait until bar 11 to take up the theme *unaccompanied*, followed immediately by the horns.

**Bars 1–39**

The second half of the principal theme, initiated in the second half of bar 5, proves to be the one that generates most of the thematic material for the movement. Its catchy rhythm ♩ ♩ ♩ ♩ ♪♪ ♩ is heard throughout, antiphonally between trumpets and horns; tutti; and extended in sequences, bouncing the music towards its strong perfect cadences. The first of these cadences is at bars 10–11 in the tonic; the next in the dominant key (A major) at bars 26–27; and the third (which, apart from its fuller scoring, mirrors the first) back in the tonic at bars 38–39. They all share the same rhythmic technique in which the natural accents in the bar are displaced: this is known as **hemiola**. The time-signature $\frac{3}{2}$ indicates that there are 3 minim beats in each bar. In a hemiola, two bars – a total of 6 minim beats – are heard as though there are three bars of 2 minim beats:

Regrouping the notes this way redistributes the normal strong and weak beats in the bar. In performance these cadences are often played with slight accents that emphasise this rhythmic displacement:

The hemiola was a common feature of English music in triple time.

**Bars 40–74** A substantial middle section follows. It begins with a reference to the rhythmic figure first heard in bar 5, but, although the three-crotchet pattern persists in the accompaniment, and there is some additional syncopation, this part of the movement has a very different character:

➢ It is in the relative minor key of B minor, with a modulation to its dominant, F♯ major, at bar 57

➢ The 1st violins have a very elaborate part (which the oboes cannot always double)

➢ A 3rd violin part has been added to thicken the harmony in the middle of the texture

➢ Trumpets and horns are silent throughout.

Until bar 66 the music is fully scored for all the instruments, but from there they gradually drop out, thinning the previously busy texture and winding down, preparing for the return of the first section of the movement.

The Italian words '*da capo*' (meaning 'from the beginning') at the end of this section indicate a repeat of the first half of the piece, sending the players back to bar 1. The finishing point of the movement has already been indicated by another Italian term '*Fine*' at bar 39. The simple structure of this otherwise elaborate piece is, therefore, ternary, A-B-A.

## Exercise 25

1. Study bars 40–66 of your score. Identify the following features:

   a. Any bar and beat where the third violin part supplies the leading-note in F♯ major.

   b. Any two-bar phrase in which the 2nd violins have a syncopated rhythm.

   c. Describe the role of the oboes in the texture in bars 40–44; 49–57; 61–64.

   d. Compare the harmonies in bars 44–49 with those in bars 57–61.

## HWV 349/13: Trumpet Minuet / Menuet (Coro)

A minuet (English) or *menuet* (French) was a popular court dance, in $\frac{3}{4}$ time. It was usually short and rhythmically straightforward. Almost all the sources agree that this piece was to be played three times: first with trumpets and strings; next with horns, oboes and bassoon(s); lastly the full band (tutti). This seems clear enough, but what happens in bars 9-12?

## Exercise 26

Listen to a recording of HWV 349/13: Trumpet Minuet / Menuet (Coro). Is it played three times? Does the scoring of each playing vary as suggested? Are bars 9–12 always played as in the score, or do they vary? Describe any variation you hear.

The Menuet is a strong movement and it is easy to understand why it might have been the very last piece of the *Water Music*. It stays firmly in the tonic key, has a strong forward-moving rhythm, a purposeful, striding bass line, and some brief moments of dissonance which also help to push it on.

> It has been suggested that the word 'Coro', which is given in some scores, indicates that Handel might have been using a pre-existent piece; probably from an opera and possibly by another composer.

In bar 1 all the instruments repeat the tonic chord, except the bassoons, cellos and basses – their C♯ immediately gives the music a feeling of moving forward. This happens again, but differently, in bar 2: the B changes the harmony to chord VI (a strong progression), and in bar 4 the lower instruments hold a B against the upper parts' repeated tonic chord. This moment in bar 4 could be explained as chord VI $^7$, but it is probably better heard (and more typically at this period) as a decorated suspension resolving (eventually) upwards onto IVb (bar $4^3$). The chords in bar 5 also form a strong progression initiating a II–V$^7$–I cadence. This striding bass line counteracts the otherwise static harmonies of the parts above it.

The harmonic interest continues in the second section, this time with passing notes *on* the beat in the upper parts. For example, in bar $10^2$ the passing-note B against the harmonising C♯ in the bass pushes the melodic line upwards; the A at bar $13^2$, and E at $14^2$ serve the same purpose on the downward scale.

The whole piece is punctuated by the drum-like rhythm in bars 7, 11, 15 and 23. (The temptation for modern performers to enhance this rhythm by adding timpani is understandable.)

Bars 17–18 and 19–20 seem to invite a contrast of $f$ and $p$. It was not normal practice, at the time that Handel was working, to notate dynamic markings, but an established convention of performing such contrasts was well understood (and is often referred to today as 'terraced dynamics').

## HWV 349/14: Lentement

All the sources agree about this title. The word '*lentement*' is not actually a title, but a French term for the tempo, meaning 'slowly'. It has been suggested that the dotted rhythm that pervades the piece is a version of a French dance movement, a slow gigue called a *loure*. It is, of course, another *da capo* ternary-form piece. It is unusual in that its middle section begins in the relative key of B minor but ends in E minor. Calling this the supertonic minor makes it sound rather a remote modulation, but it is a related key: think of it as the relative minor of the subdominant key of G.

If you worked through exercise 19 on page 65 you will already have studied the music quite closely. Look again at your answers, checking them against the score. If you didn't complete exercise 19, you would find it helpful to do so now.

## HWV 349/15

This short piece has no official title but, in several sources, an instruction that it be played three times. It is effectively another dance movement, having all the characteristics of a bourrée. It has the bourrée's defining rhythmic characteristics – it's quick, in ¢, and starts every phrase on the last crotchet of the bar. It does not modulate but, for such a quick piece, its harmonic rhythm is quite lively – mostly two chords per bar, but sometimes a different one on each crotchet (such as in bars 3 and 7).

No bassoon part is given in the Bärenreiter score; in the Eulenburg edition two bassoons are shown, doubling the cellos and basses.

---

### Exercise 27

1. In pencil, on your score:

   a. Phrase the melody of the 1st violin part.

   b. Write 'VI' under an example of a submediant chord; and 'II' under an example of a supertonic chord.

2. Looking at your score:

   a. Identify an example of a descending sequence.

   b. Compare the 2nd trumpet and 2nd horn parts at bar $5^4$–$6^4$ with the music of the rest of the orchestra. Explain which notes in the texture are harmony notes, and which are inessential notes.

---

## Reception

The most important member of the audience, the king, was evidently pleased with Handel's *Water Music* – he called for the music to be repeated on the homeward journey. Handel had struck the right note(s): impressive, almost unique sonorities, a mix of fashionable styles and pleasing tunes. Some of the pieces quickly became popular, particularly in arrangements for keyboard, and the continuing attempts to reconstruct the original order of performance indicate that, as a collection, the *Water Music* is considered to have significant musical merit.

## Interpretations and recordings

Indoor performances today (as most studio-recorded ones will be) may well add a continuo instrument (a harpsichord, or a plucked, chordal instrument such as a lute). Views differ on whether this is justified: those against arguing that Handel (deliberately) composed the music in such a way that all the harmonies are complete.

There are many different types of performance of the piece available on the internet. Listen to three or four (avoiding arrangements for other instrumental combinations), and choose *two* that sound different from one another. Get to know them both well and try to pin point what the differences are:

➤ Pitch?

➤ Tempi?

➢ Dynamics?

➢ Ornamentation?

➢ Instruments – modern, or reproductions of eighteenth century ones (period instruments)?

➢ Bowing?

➢ Articulation?

The only ornaments given in the early source used to prepare the Bärenreiter edition are short trills, and none of them are for the trumpet or horn. Performers on these instruments in Handel's day could perform some trills using a technique known as 'lip trills', using subtle changes in their embouchure. Performers using modern instruments have no difficulty trilling, helped by the pistons/valves under their left hand fingers. The Alla hornpipe movement has many trills marked for 1st violins (and 1st oboe, doubling) and they are a notable feature of its middle section. This section also has rare articulation/bowing markings: the crotchets of bars 70–71 are slurred in pairs.

> **Further reading**
>
> The Cambridge Music Handbook by Christopher Hogwood, *Handel: the Water Music and Music for the Royal Fireworks*, CUP, 2005, ISBN 978-0-521-54486-3 is a reliable guide to the background to this music.

## Mozart: Concerto E♭ major for Horn, K. 495, third movement

## Context

The concerto in Mozart's time was a substantial display piece in three movements, usually for a single soloist, with orchestral accompaniment. It was a genre that he made very much his own: as well as 27 concertos for piano, he composed others for horn, four concertos for violin, one each for flute, oboe, clarinet and bassoon and one for flute and harp.

Although Mozart played the violin and viola well, it was as a pianist that he made his reputation as a performer and many of his piano concertos were designed to show off his own talent on this still relatively new instrument. They earned him much-needed money at the series of subscription concerts that he gave in a fashionable concert venue in Vienna, the Ausgarten. He worked under pressure, often leaving some of his solo part blank, to be improvised on the day.

Some of his concertos were composed for his most talented pupils (another form of self-advertisement), but several were for friends or colleagues. The Horn Concerto, K495, was a gift for a long-standing family friend, Ignaz Leutgeb.

'K' stands for Köchel, the man who compiled the standard catalogue of Mozart's works.

## Joseph (Ignaz) Leutgeb (1732–1811)

Nothing is known about any performances of this work but, as Mozart had already composed several other pieces for Leutgeb, it must be assumed that he would not have written yet another unless at least one performance was likely. The very small size of the orchestra suggests that this concerto may have been prepared for an informal setting rather than a public or grand aristocratic occasion. Something is known, however, about the actual performer for whom the music was composed.

Leutgeb had played the horn (and violin) in the same orchestra as Mozart's father, Leopold, in Salzburg, as far back as 1763 when Mozart was a young boy. As well as playing in orchestras he had also been performing solo horn concertos in many European cities as far back as the early 1750s, including 14 times in Vienna in the 1760s. Before going to Salzburg Leutgeb had been briefly a member of Haydn's orchestra in Eszterház. In 1770 he performed in Frankfurt and Paris, as well as in Italy. An enthusiastic review of his performance in Paris in 1770 described his tone as 'mellow' and praised his ability to make the instrument 'sing' in slow movements.

The relationship between Leutgeb and Mozart seems to have been a very good-humoured one. Anecdotes about shared jokes occur frequently in biographies, some of which are supported by evidence in the composer's own letters (Mozart usually wrote Leutgeb's name as 'Leitgeb'). They remained good friends right up to Mozart's death.

## Scores

Only an incomplete autograph manuscript has survived, dated by the composer '26th June 1786'. Roughly the last half of the third movement (from bar 140) exists in Mozart's own handwriting. In this, as elsewhere in other parts of the manuscript, Mozart used differently-coloured inks – the solo horn part is in red. The exact purpose of each colour has never become clear but it is likely that they were the basis of some sort of humorous understanding between the two men. Various slightly different editions of the music were published after Mozart's death, the first in 1802.

Modern editors have tried hard to reconcile all these sources but there can be no absolutely definitive, authoritative urtext. The most reliable versions currently available are published by Bärenreiter and Henle. In the Henle score the solo part is printed in red from bar 140, following Mozart's incomplete autograph manuscript. Both these editions reflect current scholarly views. More widely available, however, may be copies of the miniature score published by Eulenburg. Whichever edition you use, you may well notice slight deviations in performances from what you see in your score.

**Bar numbers**

One problem lies in bar numbering: the Eulenburg (and its online download) have a bar-numbering glitch: its 'bar 60' is actually 'bar 50' but, by bar 70, the numbering is correct. A more significant, disconcerting difference lies in a four-bar phrase (bars 105–109) that is given once only in the Eulenburg edition but immediately repeated in the Bärenreiter and Henle scores. After bar 109, therefore, there is a four-bar difference in numbering between these scores.

OCR's specification does not require you to use any particular score. The Eulenburg score can be downloaded from imslp.org; a scanned copy of the autograph manuscript is also available on this site. The extract in the exam will not look exactly like any of these editions; whichever part of the movement it comes from, its bars will be numbered differently, starting with bar number 1.

The Eulenburg score shows the soloist continuing to play throughout all the orchestral passages, almost non-stop (e.g. bars 9–16). The more scholarly scores omit these from the soloist's part and very few performers choose to play in the tutti sections. Slightly different traditions of performing the solo part have developed among horn players and you may spot minor differences from all the scores in the performances you hear, for example, some players add an upbeat quaver an octave lower on the last quaver of bar 83, to lead into the next new melody. Mozart wrote in very few grace notes and it is not always clear which of these are intended as very short acciaccaturas or slightly longer appoggiaturas. Performers frequently add some of their own. You may also notice minor differences over slurs.

## Orchestra

Compared with those needed to play Mozart's symphonies and grandest piano concertos (or operas), this work requires a very small orchestra, and an unusual combination: strings, of course; and two oboes, but not the expected flute or bassoon; two horns instead (besides the soloist). The orchestral horn parts are unobtrusive, perhaps blending better with the sound of the solo instrument than bassoons might have done. Leutgeb's sound could be very expressive and sweet, especially in slow movements, as the Paris newspaper review indicated. The setting for this work may well have been a family drawing room, and the music performed by friends. Mozart himself made no attempt to publish it – neither he nor Leutgeb (two very hard-up musicians) appears to have made any money out of this piece.

> The following commentary gives the Eulenburg numbering first with plus-four bars in the Bärenreiter and Henle editions indicated in square brackets.

Such a small wind ensemble would not need to be matched by a large band of string players – perhaps there were just a handful? One striking feature of the string writing in the last movement, however, prompts a question: might Mozart himself have played in the orchestra? Most unusually, there is a moment where the viola line divides (bars 99–105), doubling the 1st and 2nd violins an octave below, and there are two other passages where the instrument breaks free of its conventional role of filling up the harmony (e.g. bars 61–66 and 114–119 [118–123]). It is known that Mozart often took the viola part when playing string quartets with Haydn. His fondness for the instrument is evident in his string quintets which are composed for two violins, two violas and only one cello, rather than using two cellos as was more usual.

The orchestra's role in the third movement is to:

➤ to accompany discreetly

➤ to 'punctuate' the movement with vigorous tuttis

➤ to engage in short moments of gentle dialogue, or to nudge the performer on

➤ to maintain a respectful silence when the soloist improvises a brief cadenza.

The dynamic markings are very basic: the orchestra is to be soft while the soloist plays, and loud when he doesn't. This was conventional practice in solo concertos at this time.

## Outline structure

The late-18th-century concerto was not yet the 'trial of strength' between soloist and orchestra that it tended to become in the 19th century. It was an opportunity to show off the best of the performer's technique and musicianship in an amicable, supportive relationship with the orchestra. The first movement was almost always the most substantial, the second slow and lyrical, and the last (as here) a less weighty, light-hearted rondo, usually fast and in $\frac{6}{8}$ time. All Mozart's horn concertos end with a similar movement.

The defining principle of a rondo is a (very recognisable) recurring main theme that alternates with contrasting episodes.

In the last movement of K.495 this main theme (A) always comes back in the tonic key (E♭ major) but, as was very common practice in music of this period, the first episode (B) moves towards the dominant key (B♭ major). When (B) comes back later in the movement, it modulates only briefly to the dominant, but with some rich new harmonies, and the musical material is recast to keep insisting and pointing towards the tonic key. The central episode (C), again in common with so many similar movements, begins in a closely-related key (C minor), before modulating freely.

In preparation for the examination you will need to have a secure grasp of the structure of the third movement in order to be able to explain where in the movement the score extract comes from. It can be summed up like this:

**A**    **B¹** → dominant    **A**    **C** (rel. min/modulating)    **A**    **B²** (dom. → tonic)    **A/Coda**

When you use shorthand labels like A, B or C in an examination answer *always* begin by defining what you intend them to refer to: e.g. B² is the second appearance of the first episode. You won't need to use small numbers for each return of A unless the examination extract includes its very beginning, or is the last one that merges into the coda. Apart from subtle differences in the way that Mozart joins A to the previous episode (B¹, C, or B²), A is always the same.

## Rondo theme (A) bars 1–16, E♭ major (tonic)

| Solo | 1–8 | |
|---|---|---|
| Tutti | 9–16 | (whether the soloist plays or not) |

## Episode 1 (B¹) bars 16–67

| Solo | 16–24 | E♭ major |
|---|---|---|
| | 24–38 | transition to B♭ major |
| Solo | 38–46 | B♭ major |
| Tutti | 46–48 | transition to E♭ major |
| Solo | 48–52 | transition back to B♭ major |
| Tutti | 52–54 | = bars 46–48 repeated |
| Solo | 54–68 | leading back to rondo theme: begins by repeating bars 48–49, but with changed harmony to strengthen the dominant feel. It treats the perfect cadence in B♭ (bars 59–60) as the dominant of the original tonic key; the return of A (with three quavers in place of the original one) is prepared by a sustained dominant pedal (B♭) in the bass line (bars 60–67). |

## Rondo theme (A), bars 67–83

= bars 1–16 repeated without any change

## Episode 2 (C), bars 84–121 [125]

| Solo | 84–91 | C minor |
|---|---|---|
| | 92–99 | begins as a repetition of 84–91 but turns to A♭ major (bar 96) |
| | 99–120 | solo and orchestra in quiet conversation, modulating: |
| | | C minor (relative minor) (bar 105) |
| | | G minor (relative minor of the dominant) (bar 109 [133]) |
| | | F minor (relative minor of the subdominant) (bar 114 [118]) |
| | | E♭ major (tonic) |

## Rondo theme (A), bars 121–136 [125–140]

The beginning dovetails with the end of C

## Episode 3 (B²) bars 136–178 [140–182]

| | | The answers to question 3 of exercise 28 (see page 96) give details of this passage. Do not read them until you have completed the exercise. |
|---|---|---|
| | 178 [182] | pause/cadenza |

## Rondo theme / Coda (A), bars 178–213 [182–217]

The horn begins as in bars 1–8, followed by the tutti, but this time the orchestra takes off in a series of energetic sequences (188–197) [192–201]. In a loud, busy texture (notice Mozart's careful articulation of slurs and staccato, as well as tremolo), and with very conventional harmonies, it seems to be romping towards the finishing line. It is suddenly halted by an unusual interrupted cadence: the 1st violins' E♭ is harmonised by chord V⁷b in the dominant key (bar 197 [201]). More rich harmonies accompany the soloist's next two repeats of the concluding phrase of A (197–205 [201–209]). The tonic key is finally confirmed by the soloist's descending arpeggios, the orchestra's tonic pedal in horns and bass, and undulating tonic/dominant quavers in the strings.

**Exercise 28**

1. a. On a piece of manuscript paper write out at sounding pitch the solo horn part from bar $16^6$ to $30^1$.

   b. Using a treble clef, write out the viola part from bar 61 to 66.

2. Study the whole passage from bar $16^6$ to 67 very carefully. Make detailed notes for yourself describing the following features:

   ➤ the melodic and rhythmic material

   ➤ keys, modulations and harmonies

   ➤ orchestral textures

➤ the nature of the solo part (e.g. arpeggiac or melodic? diatonic or chromatic? high or low?)

3. When you feel you know this passage (bars $16^6$ to 67) really well, turn to bars $136^6$ [$140^6$] to 178 [182] and, *without looking back*, compare them with what you have just noted in no. 2. Describe in as much detail as you can:

   a. what is the same?

   b. what is different?

   c. identify the place of this second passage in the overall structure of the movement. Don't just give it a label – give a detailed explanation

   d. briefly describe the music that follows.

Answers to this exercise can be found at the end of the Mozart section, on page 96.

## Orchestral textures

Only in the very last bars does the whole orchestra play at the same time as the soloist. All other accompanying passages are for strings alone. Short though the movement is, in each of its clearly-differentiated sections Mozart varies the scoring. For instance, in the first 40 bars:

**A:** The first eight bars are lightly accompanied every time they appear; short notes (a quaver rest after every crotchet) in a homophonic texture; simple diatonic harmony; a lively semiquaver flourish (bar 4) makes a seamless join between the two 4-bar phrases; violins and cellos/basses pick up on the solo's quaver rhythm (bars 7–8), getting ready to launch their own statement of the theme.

In the tutti at bar 8 1st and 2nd violins have the melody in octaves; violas and cellos/basses are left with the original chordal accompaniment (violas have to double-stop in bars 11–12 to complete the harmony); the notes played by the orchestral horns are very limited (as in the Handel horn parts they are mainly notes of the tonic and dominant chords) but they compensate by reinforcing the bouncy rhythm; oboes have a part each in longer notes to strengthen the harmony.

**B:** In bars 16–24 the accompaniment reverts to strings only – simple light chords, but played more rhythmically; at bar 24 they have a contrasting legato melody, thickly scored in 3rds and 6ths (violas divided); a rhythmic fragment passes backwards and forwards between soloist and orchestra before a *f* intervention (bar 36) which leads (in a strong, descending quaver passage played in octaves with oboes doubling) to the cadence that establishes the dominant key. The horns reinforce the cadence with three strong Fs (the new dominant) and the new tonic, B♭. In this way the orchestration highlights an important structural moment – the modulation to the dominant.

As you listen to the rest of the movement notice other details of scoring, particularly the interest that Mozart gives to the viola part. For example, the passing of the 2nd violin role to the viola in bars 57–58 (partnering the 1st violins a 6th below); the *divisi* from bar 99, followed at bar 110 [114] by a plangent dissonance against the bass – a dominant minor 9th, which is repeated twice as the music modulates until bar 119 [123].

**The horn**

The horn had become a very popular instrument on the continent in the first half of the 18th century. The sort of instrument in use at this time combined some of the expressive sweetness of the French type of horn, which had sparked Count von Spork's original enthusiasm, and the more rousing sounds of the German hunting horn. Many horn concertos were written by a wide range of composers (including Mozart's father). Particularly popular were double horn concertos, that is works for two horn soloists. There were a great number of very highly-skilled performers who could play melodically in its highest register. Until just after the middle of the 18th century this was usually achieved by expert 'lipping' of the notes, which is slightly altering the natural pitch by changes in embouchure.

'Bouche' is the French word for 'mouth'.

There is not always agreement among those of today's horn players who have studied the natural horn (one without valves) about the techniques needed to play it. For example, which aspects of embouchure are the most influential; the muscles of the lips; their shape; the placing of the tongue; the angle of blowing; and the nature of the mouthpiece itself.

**Hand-stopping**

In the middle of the century a new technique for altering the pitch of the natural notes was developed: hand-stopping. The hand supporting the horn was moved carefully inside the instrument's bell to affect the airflow, slightly altering the pitch (by as much as a semitone). Using this technique a greater range of notes became possible, particularly those in a lower octave than the one previously needed to play adjacent notes. Leutgeb was an expert in this technique

The aim of hand-stopping was to make more notes of the scale available to horn players. The timbre of hand-stopped notes was slightly different from the natural ones – considerable skill was required to achieve the illusion of a completely even tone – and the instrument was still more comfortable playing in the key in which it was pitched. It would not be until the invention of valves in the 19th century that a fully chromatic instrument, able to play with equal ease in any key, would be developed.

**Solo part**

In a concerto it was expected that the soloist would 'show off' the most brilliant aspects of his technique, as well as the full extent of his musicianship. When Mozart composed for other people, whether they were pupils or already professional musicians, he would tailor the music to give them an opportunity to exploit their strengths while, at the same time, avoiding exposing their weaknesses. Therefore it can be assumed that the nature of Leutgeb's solo part in this movement reflects the best of what he could manage comfortably. The highest note in his part is C (actual pitch) an octave above middle C; in other horn concertos Mozart took the solo part up to D or E♭.

The harmonic series for the natural horn would have been:

For Leutgeb's horn pitched in E♭ the natural notes would have been:

Although experiments were already under way, it was not until later that new technologies offered first piston valves, then today's rotary valves, which would make a very much wider range of notes available, including, eventually, complete chromatic scales.

These were the notes that would be readily available, and also the ones that would sound most clearly. The lively rondo theme, with its bubbling repeated notes and arpeggiac figures, was typical of traditional 'hunting horn' sounds. The technique of hand-stopping enabled Leutgeb to play more consecutive melodic notes and some chromatic ones.

Here is the full range of notes that Mozart wrote for him in this movement. The natural notes have been written in the usual way, the diamond shaped notes indicate which are natural notes but sound slightly out of tune, and the square notes are those that are hand-stopped and lipped.

**Performance technique**   Some of the most advanced displays of Leutgeb's technique are reserved for later moments in the movement, some features of which you will already have noticed.

**B²**: The horn begins this passage as a straightforward repetition of B¹, but after four bars takes a surprising turn. There are no flamboyant arpeggios or rapid notes, but the instrument is most certainly showing off: by turning to the tonic minor, a G♭ becomes necessary (bar 141 [145]). If that was not hard enough the soloist repeats the minor 3rd in bar 143 [147] but then reaches beyond his previously highest note (the dominant, B♭) a further semitone to C♭ (bar 144) [149]. The third time he settles for the B♭ but approaches it via a tricky A♮ (bar 146) [150]. To be able to reach and sustain these high notes, not once but three times, is very demanding – not only in terms of pitching difficult chromatic notes, but of stamina as well. It's almost as though the soloist was saying 'You're probably amazed by these notes but I can keep on doing this all day long', and he continues by chortling to himself on bubbly repeated notes (bars 147²–151 [151–155]).

The return to the thematic material of B at bar 153 [157] is also changed to show that there are still more tricks up his sleeve. The arpeggiac figure is turned around to reach a yet higher note than the C♭ of bar 144 [149]: C♮ in bar 154 [159]. Then, as if to say 'That's it, I've had enough of this high stuff', the horn settles on its lowest E♭ and lingers on it while the orchestra continues as though nothing exceptional has happened. But more is to come: in bars 163–168 [167–172] an energetic upward tonic arpeggio stretches up to hold the top B♭ for a whole bar (the longest note yet), following with a slow chromatic descent to G in similar dotted minims. This is followed by what sounds like a final perfect cadence. For the first time the horn part notates an appoggiatura (though you may hear other ornaments improvised elsewhere in some performances). Again, this is not final: the soloist repeats the long, slow, high notes trick and extends the chromaticism, with a reminscence of the G♭ from earlier in this episode, before reaching a dominant chord which provides the opportunity for a brief cadenza (this is usually only a flourish on the dominant chord – there isn't really any need to show off any further facets of technique). Is the cadenza, then, really the end of the fireworks?

At bar 178 [182] the soloist starts the main theme (A). This is its last appearance in its original form. The orchestra picks up as usual but wanders off course (bars 188–197 [192–201]) as though it now intends to round the movement off with a grand noise and perfect cadences. The soloist rebukes the orchestra with another go at the Rondo theme, this time its second half, as if to say 'This is what you should have done, and just to make sure I'll do it twice' (bars 201–205 [205–209]). Tweaking the orchestra's nose a little more, the soloist begins this last statement of the second half of the theme with a cheeky octave jump in place of the regular dominant-tonic anacrusis (bars 201-202 [205-206]). The orchestra subsides, repeating the final phrase (over a static tonic pedal in cellos/basses, as well as in the orchestral horns in bars 205–211 [209–215]), while the soloist, in a final burst of jubilant exuberance shows off with a downward tonic arpeggio over two octaves, from the high B♭ to the lowest note so far. Does this downward descent (in contrast with all the upward ones in the movement) signal a 'coming-to-rest'? The outline of the last three bottom notes of the horn part make a very pronounced perfect cadence by themselves: B♭–B♭–E♭. It is the horn player himself who determines when he is ready to finish.

In comparison with the virtuosic feats that were possible on other instruments, Leutgeb's part might seem on first hearing a little tame, or unadventurous. When the limitations of his instrument are borne in mind, the extent to which the soloist is the commanding figure in the movement becomes clear. The horn of the 18th century did not have the power of today's more powerful French horn – or the range and flexibility of other solo instruments like the violin and clarinet. However, Mozart has created opportunities for Leutgeb to show what he could achieve in solos that dominate the orchestral texture effectively.

Is Mozart also having fun with Leutgeb's part? Serious academics have begun to study Mozart's playfulness in other genres. Given what is known about the relationship between the two men it seems very likely that there might have been some jokiness about this final movement.

What is your response to this music? Listen to as many recordings as you can. Decide which one best fits your conception of the music. Do any of them surprise you? In what ways?

## Answers for Exercise 28

1. a.

b.

2. Principal features that you might have noticed include:

a new melody for the horn in a balanced 8-bar phrase; a short rhythmic figure which gradually extends; a continuation of the new melody (at bar 43), followed by a strong upward broken chord phrase which is repeated (bar 54) and its rhythmic figure extended; a dotted minim chromatic descent leading back to the main Rondo theme (A).

begins in the tonic; begins to modulate, via F major, and sequentially over part of the circle of 5ths, at bar 25; F major becomes the dominant of the real dominant, B♭, at bar 36; B♭ bass line from bar 60 becomes a dominant pedal in the tonic key (E♭) from bar 65 (the first clue is the A♭ in the viola part).

Bars 16–24: strings only, homophonic accompaniment

Bars 24²–28: 1st violin sequential melody, 2nd violins mostly a 3rd below, doubled an octave lower by divided violas

Bars 36–38: unison strings plus oboes and orchestral horns in brief tutti, $\boldsymbol{f}$, in a descending pattern

Bars 42–46¹: 1st and 2nd violins echo the solo horn over a sustained dominant bass

Bars 46–48: tutti again, lower strings continuing the descending pattern from earlier, upper strings in strong, triple-stopped chords, oboes and horns reinforcing (the latter rhythmically as well)

Bars 60–67: dominant pedal, viola's independent part, upper strings beginning to hint at the Rondo theme in 3rds, ending with two bars marked (by Mozart) staccato.

Bars 16–24: mostly broken chords, rhythm less lively than previously

Bars 24–36: short fragment in dialogue with orchestra introduces A♮ and E♮ (bars 28–29)

Bars 38–52: mainly broken tonic/dominant chords, ending with a complete scale of B♭ major (i.e. with A♮) at bars 50–52

Bars 62–65: sustained dotted minims descending chromatically – B♭, A♮, A♭, G.

Total range = from E♭ below middle C to B♭ above.

3.  a. and b. similarities and differences:

First four bars the same 136–140 [140–144], but the second phrase is repeated with a G♭, making the music minor; soloist stretches up to the highest note so far – C♭.

Much is omitted, cutting out the modulatory passage, reaching the dominant key very quickly and turning away immediately at bar 151 [154] with the orchestra's tutti intervention from bar 46.

The entire passage from bar 38–67 is then recast to remain mostly in the tonic, and eventually tonic minor, but with virtuosic changes to the solo part: in bars 157–161 [161–165] the horn plays rhythmically in the background on a low tonic pedal; in bar 167 [171] it reaches its highest note in the piece, C natural, and an appoggiatura is added at the cadence in the next bar; when the seven bars (163–169 [167–173]) are repeated at bar 171 [175] the long chromatic notes descend onto G♭ (bar 175 [179]), followed by F♭; the strings underneath these two notes provide harmonies in the key of E♭ minor – chord VI (C♭ major) in an interrupted cadence, then the 1st inversion of the chord F♭, before chord Ic (2nd inversion E♭ minor) comes to rest on the dominant.

c.  This is the second, altered, appearance of the first Episode (B²); it has been shortened and altered to be more in the tonic key.

d.  The soloist plays a brief cadenza and leads back to the principal theme and Coda.

## Beethoven: Symphony No. 5 in C minor, Op.67, first movement

### First performance

Beethoven had waited a long time for exactly the right venue for the first performance of both his Fifth and Sixth Symphonies: at last the director of the Imperial Theatre in Vienna agreed a date for his benefit concert, 22nd December 1808. The daily newspaper announced that it would consist of entirely new music, 'not yet heard in public'. It was to be a marathon programme:

**Part 1:**  What we now know as the Symphony No. 6 (*Pastoral*) but was referred to at this performance as the No. 5

An aria (in the event, a favourite one that Beethoven had composed much earlier was performed)

A sacred piece with Latin text 'composed in the church style with chorus and solos'

Piano Concerto No. 4, with Beethoven himself as soloist

**Part 2:**  'Grand Symphony in C minor' (billed as the Sixth, later known as the Fifth)

Another sacred piece with Latin text

Fantasia for piano solo

Another Fantasia 'for the Pianoforte which ends with the gradual entrance of the entire orchestra and ends with the introduction of choruses as a finale'

There was time for only one, very inadequate rehearsal and arrangements were generally chaotic. The last piece, the *Choral Fantasia*, had not been finished until the very last moment and it was no surprise that there were mistakes on the night which caused Beethoven to stop the orchestra and restart the performance. This caused a great deal of resentment – even before the concert he was known to be on bad terms with his orchestra.

It was a very long evening (6.30–10.30pm). One member of the audience, invited to share a box with one of Beethoven's patrons, Prince Lobkowitz, complained how cold it was, and wrote that he had 'experienced the truth that one can easily have too much of a good thing – and still more of a loud'. The many mistakes upset them on the composer's behalf: 'Poor Beethoven, who from this, his own concert, was having the first and only scant profit that he could find in a whole year, had found in the rehearsals and performance a lot of opposition and almost no support'.

In a letter to his publishers the following month Beethoven acknowledged that mistakes had been made, 'which I could not help', but believed the audience had been enthusiastic.

## The score

The instrumental parts for the symphony were published the following year, in April 1809. Having heard the music in performance, Beethoven wished to make some amendments to the manuscript he had sent to the publishers earlier: one of these was to extend the D in bar 4 by a further bar (and at all the equivalent places throughout the score). His instruction arrived too late for inclusion in the first printed edition, but many amendments were made in subsequent editions. His original manuscript is in the State Library in Berlin: it shows detailed instructions to the copyist and many second thoughts and crossings-out.

If you are using an Eulenburg edition you will find some terms are given in German: '*zu 2*' (in bar 1) means that both instruments play the same part. The keys in which horns and clarinets are pitched is also given in German: 'Clarinetti in B' are clarinets in B♭, and 'Corni in Es' are horns in E♭.

The metronome marking was added later on in Beethoven's lifetime: there is almost unanimous agreement among conductors that it indicates a speed far faster than he really intended. In the recordings that you hear compare the speed of the whole-bar beat in the opening bars, the length of the pauses, and whether the beat after the pauses is the same as the one before.

# Sonata form (1st movement form)

Below is a summary of its structure:

(Introduction)  **EXPOSITION**  :‖  **DEVELOPMENT**  **RECAPITULATION**  (Coda)

An introduction or coda was optional. Although introductions were not very common, most composers rounded off with a short coda. Beethoven extended its significance (and length) considerably.

The names of the sections convey the broad idea. The detail of what went on in each of them was usually:

**Exposition:**  A first subject (theme) in the tonic (A)

Transition to the dominant (or relative major if A is in a minor key)

One or more themes in the new key = the second subject or second subject group (B)

The exposition almost always ended in the dominant (or relative major) key, with a repeat sign. Conductors of orchestras today vary in their attitudes to repeating the exposition material – many choose not to.

**Development:**  Here, composers could play with the themes presented in the Exposition, or even introduce new ones. They often took fragments of a theme, extending or shortening them, passing them from instrument to instrument (textures could become imitative or even contrapuntal). Most of all, the music would almost certainly modulate, sometimes several times, and could go to quite remote keys. Eventually, when the moment came to return to a more ordered handling of the material, the return of the tonic key would be prepared, often by means of a dominant pedal.

To 'develop' a theme is not the same as to 'vary' one, though there are some techniques in common, such as using different instruments, but in a Development section wide-ranging modulation is expected. However, Beethoven does not confine developing his themes only to that named section. The process gets underway almost immediately at the beginning of the movement when he takes the opening rhythmic motif and embeds it in the texture throughout the exposition. Nor does he stop developing his material when the music reaches the recapitulation.

**Recapitulation**: First subject (A), as before, in the tonic. (Scoring and dynamics might differ.)

Transition – might give the illusion of modulating but would be altered to end in the tonic

> In the last 30 years of the 18th century, the nature of the symphony had gradually consolidated: a piece for orchestra only, it was usually in four movements, the first of which was in a form that became known as 'First Movement' or 'Sonata' Form.

Second subject (B), now in the tonic key. (A movement in a minor key might now be in the tonic major.)

**Coda:**   Literally a 'tail' added on at the end – an afterthought. Beethoven sometimes treated it as though it was a second development, making it a thoroughly integral part of the whole structure.

In his Symphony No. 5 in C minor, Beethoven cast his first movement in a very compressed version of this form. The opening rhythm ♪ ♩ pervades the movement: it is present throughout the transitions and the second subject group, and still dominates the landscape right to the very end of the coda. It might seem that such tight unity could make it difficult to know where the sections begin and end, but they are all very clear. If you learn to recognise the musical landmarks that characterise them you should have no difficulty identifying which of the sections the short extract that you will be given in the examination comes from.

## Outline Structure

**Exposition (bars 1–124)**

Bars 1–21   First subject (A) – tonic (C minor)

Bars 22–52   Continuation (Beethoven is already developing) - remaining in the tonic

Bars 52–58   A very abrupt transition (the surprise chord in bar 52 is a diminished 7th chord – one which can be ambiguous in its key – Beethoven prepares his modulation with it)

Bars 59–110   Second subject group (B) – relative major (E♭ major).

The most prominent feature of this group of themes is its opening: two horns in unison in bars 59-62 (B$^1$), which seems to have grown out of A, but with the falling interval (of bars 1–2) stretched from a 3rd to a 5th. The contrasting 1st violin melody in bars 63–94 (B$^2$) never manages to shake off the rhythm of A which persists stubbornly (almost like an ostinato) in the bass line. In a third idea at bar 94, a tutti surge swirls towards perfect cadences (bars 110–122) which hammer home the new key (it had been briefly undermined by a chromatic creeping upwards from bar 84). The tenuous second subject of bar 63 has been completely swamped by the rhythmic figure from A. Two bars of silence must follow before going on, or repeating the exposition.

**Development (bars 125–248)**   Beethoven never lets go of his principal idea (A): in bars 125–179 the section begins and grows rather like it did at the opening, then it announces itself dressed as B$^1$, with the falling 5th (bars 179–182). After three times in different keys (G major, bars 179–187; C major, bars 187–195; F minor, bar 195), the idea is subjected to drastic surgery. Its two minims are separated from the first part of the theme (bars 197–198), treated antiphonally, and cut again so that only one minim of $B^1$ is left (bar 210). The pitch creeps up chromatically from B♭ to D♮. (Notice the moment in bars 215–216 when D♭ in the woodwind is answered enharmonically by first violins on C♯).

'Enharmonic' is a term for a note that is spelled two or more ways, such as C♯ or D♭.

This D♮ seems to satisfy Beethoven and, after a mysteriously quiet passage, he allows the full theme to get going again. This time, however, it is with two falling 3rds (not a 5th) and a lingering thought about cutting it all up again (bar 233) and a single chord is repeated from bar 238 to 248$^1$. Functioning like a dominant pedal, it prepares the listener's ear for the return of the tonic key to begin the recapitulation.

If you worked through exercise 24 on page 76, you will already have studied Beethoven's handling of dynamic extremes in the development section; it culminates in A, in the tonic key, played (*ff*) by the full orchestra at bar 248. It is by this well-judged use of dynamics and instrumentation (and rhythm) that Beethoven arrives, seamlessly, at the beginning of the next section.

**Recapitulation (bars 248-374)**

| | |
|---|---|
| Bars 248 (2nd quaver)–268 | First subject (A) – tonic (C minor), rescored. A short oboe cadenza fills out the original pause and 2-bar silence of the exposition, highlighting this structural moment. |
| Bars 269–292 | As before, but this time Beethoven doesn't exit from the diminished 7th chord in bars 296–300 onto the dominant of E♭ major (as in the exposition). Instead he reaffirms the tonic key, C minor, with its dominant chord (bar 302). |
| Bars 303–374 | Second subject group as before but re-engineered (and rescored) to stay in the tonic key, C minor, and eventually sidestepping into the tonic major, C major (from bar 340). |

**Coda (bars 374 – 502)**

Tutti: the principal rhythmic idea is shared across the full orchestra: tonic major, swerving immediately towards F minor (the subdominant key) in bars 376–386. Beethoven continues developing material until the point where he appears to be about to repeat the recapitulation (bars 478–482). However, an open fifth in the cellos (bars 484–491) forms a quiet but very stable tonic pedal. Then 12 bars of perfect cadences in the tonic announce the end of the first movement.

## Orchestration

The 'line-up' in this movement is more typical of orchestras of the late 18th/early 19th century when compared to Mozart's very small orchestra for his Horn Concerto No. 4:

➢ Double woodwind (two each of flutes, oboes, clarinets in B♭ and bassoons)

In the last movement of this symphony Beethoven enlarged the orchestra, adding a piccolo, a contrabassoon and three trombones. This increased the overall pitch range and dynamic power.

➢ 2 horns (in E♭)

➢ 2 trumpets (in C)

➢ Timpani (tuned to the tonic and dominant notes, C and G)

➢ Strings (1st and 2nd violins, violas, cellos and basses.

The sounds Beethoven created with this combination, however, were not typical. He was very alert to subtle differences of timbre between instruments, and, in other pieces he would choose individual ones to play solo melodies because of their distinctive tone colours. In this movement, though, there are only very brief moments where a particular instrument is used in this way.

**'Solo' moments**

➢ In bars 59–62, when the two horns (***ff***) announce B$^1$

➢ In bars 67–70 when the 1st clarinet picks up B$^2$ from the 1st violins (and also from 130–135 when both clarinets in unison 'answer' the strings, echoing the violas' notes an octave higher)

➢ In bar 268 where the 1st oboe is singled out for a reflective cadenza during the pause

➢ In bars 303–306 when both bassoons in unison restate B$^1$ (but are they chosen to do this, not because of their tone colour, but because the horns can't manage it in the new key (C minor) and the theme lies comfortably in their range? Modern conductors occasionally replace them with valve horns – listen carefully to various recordings.)

➢ In bars 311–330 when the 1st flute takes the clarinet's earlier role in dialogue with the strings

➢ Timpani are also used alone, to play the rhythmic motif, at several quiet moments such as bars 313–4.

## Dynamics

The build up to a very loud sound at the opening of the recapitulation is a typical feature of Beethoven's music. There are several crescendos like this, usually designed to work towards a strong moment (something not found in either the Handel or Mozart scores). He was also fond of sudden contrasts, often between extremes, for example bars 374–395:

➢ Bars 374–386 are scored almost for full orchestra, marked ***ff***. Notice the liberal use of **sf**, another of Beethoven's typical fingerprints. Why, though, are trumpets and timpani left out in bars 382–386? Does it have something to do with the 1st inversion chord of D♭s that is being pounded?

➢ The hushed answer in bars 387–388 is given to clarinets, horns and bassoons in unison ***p.***

➢ Bars 390–395 include trumpets and timpani on another dramatic, loud chord (they could play repeated Cs).

# Texture

When the orchestra plays tutti, Beethoven distributes the notes of a chord in a fairly typical way – notice similarities with Handel. Look again at bars 390–395:

➢ Flutes double the upper notes of the first and second violins' double-stops

➢ 2nd oboe doubles their lower note (E♭), 1st oboe doubles the A♮ of the 1st bassoon and violas, but two octaves higher

➢ Clarinets play C and A♮

➢ Bassoons play A♮ and F♯ (doubling the cellos and basses).

The chord is distributed across the whole orchestra but is also complete, and balanced within the woodwind group: each instrument plays at a pitch that is comfortable for their *ff*. Beethoven was restricted in the notes that he could give 1st and 2nd violins by the double-stopping combinations that they could manage on their four strings: he wanted the 3rd (E♭ and C) at the very top - notes that they would have to play on their highest string, E. Only one note at a time could be played on a single string so the two notes had to be shared between the 1st and 2nd violins.

Horns and trumpets also have very comfortable notes that are right in the middle of the whole texture: E♭ and C. Notice, however, how very widely spaced the strings are: there is a large gap between violins and the bass line, with violas alone in the middle on their A. Beethoven bridges this gap by bringing the lower strings up an octave at bar 391. After the opening three-quaver figure, woodwinds and brass then sustain their chord, while strings keep 'scrubbing' at theirs (the tremolo sign indicates repeated quavers throughout these bars).

Woodwind and brass may also punctuate the texture, as in bars 356–362. Here the upper strings are busy with descending quavers, lower strings stride upwards in crotchets, and the rest of the band plays off-beat chords.

There is much in the orchestration, therefore, that is typical of all three of our composers, but is used to more powerful, dramatic effect by Beethoven than had previously been heard. There is also a great deal of imaginative subtlety, as you will see in the next exercise.

## Exercise 29

Compare the texture of the orchestral writing in bars 6–15, 253–262, and 483–491 in the first movement of Beethoven's Symphony No. 5.

## Harmony

Beethoven was working roughly 20 years after Mozart composed his Horn Concerto K. 495, and almost a century after Handel composed the *Water Music* (in 1717). All three composers used what was called tonal language, based on major and minor keys and a sense of relatedness. Languages evolve all the time and you will have noticed already that Mozart's harmonic vocabulary contains chords that are not to be found in Handel's work. The introduction of chromatic notes into a chord alters its flavour, creating a 'richer' sound, but the use of several chromatic chords can undermine the sense of key. Using chromatic harmony, Beethoven extends these techniques to a point where many of his chords are deliberately ambiguous.

The harmonic vocabulary that you are required to show you can handle in Section A of the Composing Unit consists only of *diatonic* chords, that is chords that belong to the tonic key. This includes learning to modulate to closely-related keys (such as tonic to dominant and back), often using pivot chords that are common to both keys, but it does not include chords that contain chromatic notes. When you listen to your Mozart and Beethoven movements and study their scores you will hear several chromatic chords of a kind that were being used increasingly at the end of the 18th century. You are *not required* to use these in your own harmony exercises, but you will find it helpful to recognise them in the orchestral scores, to understand how they are formed and their effect, and to know their names.

Some of these chromatic chords are often used to increase ambiguity (of key). They are treated rather like the pivot chords that you are learning to use but, because they contain notes that don't belong either to the key the music is coming from, or the one it is going towards (i.e. they are chromatic notes) they arouse interest, and can cause some instability.

**Dominant minor 9ths**   Just as a 7th can be added to chord V, other notes can be piled on top (all the way to a 13th above the root). The most common interval to add was a minor 9th, as Mozart does in the last movement of his Horn Concerto, K. 495. In the sequence of viola minor 9ths on the first note of each of bars 110 [114], 114 [118], 118 [122] they are unprepared and resolved downwards, rather like some appoggiaturas. Their length makes them so prominent in the harmony that it is hard to hear them as inessential notes. The sequence takes a segment of the circle of 5ths.

**Diminished 7ths**   These were exceedingly common chords (and occurred in Handel's day although not in Suite No. 2 from the *Water Music*). The chord consists of four notes, each a minor 3rd above its neighbour. It can be thought of in two ways: either as VII[7] in a minor key, or as a dominant minor 9th that omits the root. Strange as the second explanation sounds, it was the most common explanation in the 19th century and, because it was very frequently quitted as though it had been a dominant chord, quite sensible. Because every one of the intervals that makes it up is the same (a minor 3rd) it is very easily invertible.

Beethoven used the diminished 7th chord a great deal, especially when writing in a minor key. Notice how the first example in bars 53–56 is spelled: its root is not C, but A♮ (with C, E♭ and G♭); it has grown out of a tonic chord (bar 51²) in which G is altered to G♭ (bar 52) and the A♮ then added (bar 53). This turns the key away from C minor, towards the relative key of E♭ major by quitting the diminished 7th as the dominant (minus its root – a hypothetical F) of the new dominant chord.

Compare the equivalent passage in the recapitulation (bars 296–312). The perfect cadence in the tonic key at bars 295-296 is again interrupted by a diminished 7th chord. Compare the spelling –  F♯ (not G♭), A♮, C and E♭. It sounds the same as the one in the exposition but the different spelling (which we can see but cannot hear) places it as a dominant in G major,   (chord V of V in the tonic key – the missing root would be D). There has been an illusion of modulating but the key has remained the same.

Mozart's example comes in a quieter, more reflective context at bar 202 [206], on the 2nd beat: A♮ with C, E♭ and G♭ above (the missing root is again an F). It might well have resolved onto chord V (B♭) in the tonic key, like Beethoven's first example above, especially so near the end of the movement. However, Mozart slides all the parts down a semitone (bar 203 [207]) onto yet another diminished 7th chord. The whole passage from bar 198 [202] to 205 [209] is a remarkable demonstration of the expressive use of chromatic chords. The soloist's tune is very definitely in the tonic key (E♭) but it is reharmonised with a secondary dominant (bar 198–199), minor inflections (G♭ and C♭ in bars 201–202 [205–206]) and these two diminished 7ths.

## Augmented 6th chords

Augmented 6th chords were often used by Mozart and Beethoven at important imperfect cadences, which resolve on to the dominant chord.

Beethoven uses it in this conventional way in both the exposition and recapitulation at the strong cadence that halts the first statement of his first subject material (bars 20 and 267). The augmented 6th interval lies between the lowest note, A♭, and the F♯ in the middle of the texture.

Mozart's only augmented 6th in the last movement of his Horn Concerto K. 495 is less conventional. In bar 145 [149] the augmented 6th creeps in as a barely audible slip down by the 2nd violins from C♭ in the previous chord (a chord of C♭ major) onto A♮. It is held, with an expressive quaver figure in the 1st violins in the next bar, and resolves onto the dominant chord.

## Neapolitan 6th chords

Neapolitan 6th chords were often used as chromatic colouring in the early 18th century. This is a first inversion of a chromatically-altered (flattened) supertonic chord, always almost used immediately before a Ic–V–I progression. Although it was a common chord in Handel's time there are no examples in your Handel score. Beethoven uses it twice in the first movement of Symphony No. 5, the second time rather ambiguously.

In the passage in the Beethoven score starting at bar 374 the key seems to be tonic major (C major). The chord in bar 378 can be heard either as Ib or as Vb of the next chord, IV (F minor). In which of these keys is the first inversion chord of D♭ major in bars 382–386? The moment is startling and ambiguous: the chord is either a Neapolitan chord in C major/minor or VIb in F minor. In the following two bars the clarinets, bassoons and horns, seem to ask the question (quietly) 'Which key do you really mean – C minor or F minor?'. The answer is a thundering diminished 7th (the one discussed above, with F♯). C minor is the answer and, with hindsight, it seems that the D♭ chord was a Neapolitan 6th.

## Reception

The immediate reception of Beethoven's Symphony No. 5 was mixed. Many eye- and ear-witness accounts reported that the performance was flawed (to say the least), and the extreme length of the programme left the audience with a great deal to take in. Time was needed for reflection. Subsequent performances in other German cities, and more widely across Europe, were better rehearsed. Reviews became increasingly positive, particularly among the more forward-thinking critics of the day. After a performance in Leipzig in January 1809, the editor of the local newspaper described the first movement of the Fifth Symphony as 'a very serious, somewhat gloomy yet fiery allegro, noble both in feeling and in the working-out of idea, which is handled firmly and evenly, simply with a lot of originality, strength and consistency – a worthy movement which offers rich pleasure even to those who cling to the old way of composing a big symphony.'

If you search the internet for this symphony you will find many sites that give extensive biographies of the composer, commentaries on the music, and discuss what, if anything, the contributors think it means. www.favorite-classical-composers.com, for example, allows you to hear and compare details of different conductors' interpretations.

That Beethoven intended something 'ground-breaking' was clear. His music was making a very public, personal statement. What it 'meant', and how it was to be subsequently interpreted, have been the source of many earnest discussions. His first biographer, Schindler (a pupil and later secretary of the composer) claimed that Beethoven told him that the opening bars were 'Fate knocking at the door'. However, many of Schindler's anecdotes have turned out to be the products of a faulty memory and he is not regarded as a reliable source. Several 19th-century commentators constructed imaginative narratives and interpretations often crept into later novels. The Norton edition of Symphony No. 5 has a number of appendices which may give you some idea of the profound impression this work has made ever since its first performance. Whether it 'means' anything, and what that might be, is for you to decide for yourself.

# Jazz recordings

## Instrumental jazz, 1920–1960

At the beginning of the 1920s jazz was beginning to establish itself as a distinctive style of music. Musicians from New Orleans, the birthplace of jazz, were being drawn to the big cities of America, especially New York and Chicago, and the new technologies of recording and radio broadcasting were beginning to spread the sound of jazz throughout the United States and all over the world.

By 1960, the era in which jazz had often dominated popular music was over. There had been many rapid changes in the intervening 40 years – new musical styles had travelled far and caught on quickly. Compare this with the slower development of musical ideas in the 18th and 19th centuries, when Handel, Mozart and Beethoven were composing.

This is not the same as saying that jazz itself was over by 1960! Jazz standards continue to be played and new jazz performers continue to develop their styles.

Although jazz changed rapidly, you should not assume that later styles were better than earlier ones. Although we tend to talk of music 'developing', this means only that one style tended to grow out of another in sequence. There's no reason to suppose that Miles Davis is 'better' than the New Orleans Rhythm Kings simply because he was working 30 years later. All of the jazz musicians you will be studying were among the best of their day, working with the styles and techniques of the time.

### Listening to the jazz recordings

Try to get copies of the specified recordings for each of the three works you will be studying (see the list on page 69). Take your time to get to know each work well. Jazz can seem confusing when you first hear it, but repeated listening will help you to make sense of the music. Discussing what you hear with others and working through the sections in this book will also help you.

In the exam you will only have an extract from the recording to work from. There will be no score to follow. In this book the structure of each work is laid out in a table, with the timing in minutes and seconds. There are also some musical examples, which are transcribed from the recordings.

The transcriptions are only a guide. Jazz scores are not as reliable as classical scores as it is impossible to notate all of the nuances of pitch and rhythm heard in jazz. Many jazz composers use only outline instrumental parts and communicate many of their ideas verbally. Improvised sections in your set works were not written down. You will need to listen carefully to hear how the recorded performance differs from what is written. The tables and examples are there to help you to get to know the work better.

Once you know your way around the work, put the examples and timings aside. Getting to know the work by ear is vital.

## Key features of jazz

**Frontline.** These are the instruments that play the melody line. New Orleans jazz of the 1920s used trumpet, clarinet and trombone. The saxophone overtook the clarinet in popularity in the 1930s.

**Rhythm section.** This usually consists of drums, piano, banjo (or guitar in later jazz) and bass. The bass was usually a double bass played pizzicato (plucked) although the more powerful sound of a tuba was often used on early recordings. Sometimes the left hand of the pianist provides the bass. Chords are played by the piano and banjo or guitar. Players would often fill out the harmonies by adding extra notes, fills and syncopated rhythms – a technique called comping (an abbreviation of 'accompanying').

> The bass in the earliest jazz tended to be in two-beat rhythm, reflecting its ragtime and march origins. The fourbeat pattern developed with the rise of the double bass as the main bass instrument.

**Walking bass.** A bass part, usually improvised, of four steady crotchets per bar, in which chord notes are often linked by passing notes to produce mainly stepwise movement. Earlier examples, from the late 1930s, are often quite simple but by the 1950s bass players were getting more adventurous in exploring the different registers of the instrument, giving their bass lines a character that matched the changing moods of the music as a whole.

**Improvisation.** The ability to make up and vary passages while performing, rather than reading them note by note from a copy, is an essential skill for a jazz musician. Improvisation often involves some degree of preparation of basic ideas and, in jazz, is usually based on an underlying chord pattern.

**Arrangement.** Not all jazz is improvised. Most of the works you are studying have an element of pre-composition. A jazz musician would need to be able to read music to make a living playing in the clubs and theatres of New York or Chicago. Written arrangements helped to improve standards of ensemble in the bigger bands.

**Swing.** Jazz is well known for its exciting rhythms. Early jazz reflected the syncopations of ragtime. In the 1920s, jazz musicians started replacing pairs of even quavers (known as **straight eights**) with a more lilting style in which the first quaver of each pair is held longer than the second. In addition, notes would often be anticipated or delayed in relation to the strictly maintained beat of the rhythm section. Swing is difficult to define or notate, and not everyone will agree whether a performance is swung or not.

> Basing variations on a repeating chord structure is a composing technique that has been used for centuries. In jazz, the practice of borrowing just the chords of a standard, without the tune, developed originally as a way to avoid infringing the copyright of the popular song being used.

**Changes.** Many jazz pieces are based on a repeating chord pattern known as the changes. Each repetition of the chord progression is known as a **chorus**. One of the best-known changes is the chord pattern of the 12-bar blues. Others are often based on the harmonies of well-known popular songs of the time, known as **standards**, many of which are in 32-bar song form (AABA).

**Blue notes and inflections.** Listen out for small alterations in the pitch of notes. The most common are blue notes, involving a slight flattening of the 3rd, 5th or 7th degree of the scale. A keyboard instrument gives a poor impression of how these should sound. Listen to a jazz wind player or singer and see if you can hear the pitch of certain notes being pushed higher or lower for expressive effect. The pitch can also be bent while a note is being played.

**Tone quality.** Jazz musicians use many ways to vary the sound of their instruments, including different types of attack, production (such as deliberately rough or breathy tone), and vibrato (early jazz players used a fast vibrato, but the later works you are studying have slower vibrato). Mutes are often used to change the sound of brass instruments. Originally a mute could be a piece of cloth, a hat or any item which came to hand. The most common mutes today are the straight, cup, Harmon and plunger.

**Double time.** Playing in semiquavers instead of the usual quavers.

## Recording technology

By 1920 the gramophone record had become the main way of bringing music to a wider audience, although it was soon to be joined by the newly developing medium of radio broadcasting. Recording companies spurred on the development of jazz by competing to search out new music and find artists who would be commercially successful.

Recording for the gramophone was originally an acoustic process, involving the use of a large recording horn that would capture the vibrations of the sound and record them as patterns on a wax disc. This would then be used to produce a mould from which multiple copies could be stamped onto brittle discs made from a naturally occuring compound called shellac. A shellac record was limited to three minutes of music on each side, which forced musicians to organise their pieces more compactly than they would in a live situation.

These early acoustic recordings suffered from problems of musical balance. The soloist(s) had to be placed close to the recording horn to be heard, and drums and bass instruments were difficult to record adequately – hence the reason why a tuba often replaced the double bass in the early years of recording.

Following the development of the first microphones suitable for music, electrical recording rapidly replaced the older acoustic method after 1925. The earliest works you are studying benefitted from this new process, although the end product was still a shellac disc with limited play time. Microphones improved in quality, and were soon able to cope with the bigger bands of the 1930s.

The development of tape recording and the LP (long-playing) record in the late 1940s revolutionised the record industry. Each side of an LP record offered at least 20 minutes of uninterrupted playing time, allowing jazz musicians to develop their ideas over a much longer period. Tape recording was equally revolutionary, since it became possible to edit and splice together sections recorded at different times, rather than always having to capture a complete performance in a single take. Furthermore, sound engineers could exercise better control of recording conditions, placing individual microphones in different positions so that the performance could be artificially balanced. This allowed instrumental combinations which would not be practical in a live situation. The work of the sound engineer also became increasingly important with the advent of stereo recording in the 1950s, towards the end of our period.

Securing a recording contract became an increasingly important part of the business of making jazz. Record sales generated larger audiences to hear live performances, which in turn offered the chance to secure bigger contracts with other companies later.

**Further reading**

*Jazz* by Mervyn Cooke. Thames and Hudson, 1998, ISBN 978-0-500203-18-7. A short, attractively presented guide to the history of jazz.

*Jazz Styles: History and Analysis* by Mark C. Gridley. Pearson, 2012, ISBN 978-0-20503683-7 A detailed introduction to jazz written for American college students. CDs are available separately to accompany the latest edition.

*What to listen for in Jazz* by Barry Kernfeld. Yale University Press, 1995, ISBN 978-0-30007259-4. Looks at musical elements of jazz, with a range of examples on an accompanying CD.

*A New History of Jazz* by Alyn Shipton. Continuum, 1988/2007, ISBN 978-0-82642972-8. An excellent and readable history.

This is one of the three jazz recordings set for exams in June 2014.

If you are sitting the exam in June 2015 or later, turn to the section starting on page 130.

Turn to page 144 for notes about exam questions on the jazz recordings.

# Louis Armstrong: *Hotter Than That*

Trumpeter Louis Armstrong (1901–1971) is a key figure among the New Orleans musicians who pioneered jazz. Like many other musicians, he left New Orleans as a young man for the wider opportunities of the northern cities of the United States. Initially he went to play for his mentor King Oliver in Chicago. Until the depression of the 1930s Chicago rivalled New York for theatre and cabaret (most of these establishments were run by organised crime); there was plenty of work for talented jazz musicians.

Armstrong enjoyed a successful period in New York with the Fletcher Henderson Orchestra, attracting much attention as a soloist. In 1925 Armstrong's wife, Lil Hardin, brought him back to Chicago with the promise of a job in Bill Bottoms' Dreamland Café. He was paid $75 a week: an unusually large wage at the time for a black musician.

As a band soloist at the Dreamland Café, Armstrong led a busy life. In the afternoon, for the black audiences at the Vendome Theatre, there would be an overture from the whole band, followed by music to accompany a silent movie. A solo spot would then follow in the interval: usually a jazz number, or sometimes an arrangement of an operatic aria. The evening Dreamland cabaret included music for a floor show and for dancing, usually standards or numbers from Broadway shows. Most of the work was accompanying, but Armstrong's solo improvisations attracted the admiration of many Chicago musicians.

## Hot Five and Hot Seven recordings

For Lil Hardin, having her husband with her in Chicago meant that she was both promoting his career and preventing his womanising (which had been a problem for her while Armstrong had been away in New York). Together as musicians, Armstrong and Hardin worked on much of the material for the Hot Five recordings, produced for the OKeh Phonograph Corporation.

As the Hot Five and Hot Seven recordings progressed, Armstrong's solo role increased. His performance became the focus of the recordings and an important factor in their commercial success. The key features of his style which made an impact on audiences were:

➢ His skill and resourcefulness at improvising, combining both interesting melodic detail and a satisfying overall shape

➢ His use of swing and rhythmic displacement, using rubato and cross rhythms much more freely than other contemporaries

➢ His ability to colour individual notes with vibrato, shakes, rips and falls, which gave his playing tremendous energy

➢ His trumpet technique, which employed a powerful tone and wide range

➢ His bold, dramatic solos that dominated the ensemble and enhanced his role as a virtuoso soloist

➢ His scat singing (improvised vocal solos to nonsense words).

Despite the popularity of their recordings, the Hot Five did not perform live. The players were selected from among the best of the New Orleans musicians working in Chicago. Like Armstrong they were steeped in the New Orleans style and had played in many of the same bands, including Fate Marable's Riverboat Band, Kid Ory's own band in New Orleans, and with King Oliver in Chicago. For *Hotter Than That* Armstrong added the blues guitarist Lonnie Johnson, who had won a talent competition with OKeh and was a staff musician with the company.

Armstrong had already been recording with a larger group, promoted as the Hot Seven. For this line-up of seven the rhythm section included a tuba and drums, which gave a stronger accompaniment to his solos. However, in *Hotter Than That* there is no percussion and the bass is divided between the trombone and the left hand octaves of the piano.

The main focus of the piece is on Armstrong as soloist and in his duets with Johnson (on blues guitar). There are substantial solos from Dodds and Ory. The New Orleans style of **collective improvisation** is confined to the introduction and the second half of the final chorus.

## Structure

The composition of *Hotter Than That* is credited to Lil Hardin. However, her original melody is lost and we are left with the arrangement as heard in the recording. The 32-bar chord pattern for each chorus is based on part of *Tiger Rag*, a standard for New Orleans players. Only primary chords are used to begin with: E♭ major, B♭⁷ and A♭. Note in the following extract how infrequently the chords change: E♭ for six bars, followed by B♭⁷ for eight bars, then E♭ for eight bars. By contrast the harmonic rhythm of the last eight bars is much faster, with a change of chord every four beats to drive the music forward to the end of the chorus.

### Armstrong's style

**Further listening**

Try to listen to other recordings by Louis Armstrong and the Hot Five, for example *Alligator Crawl*.

*Hotter Than That*, recorded 13 December 1927 in Chicago for OKeh by Louis Armstrong and his Hot Five.

Trumpet/vocal: Louis Armstrong

Trombone: Edward 'Kid' Ory

Clarinet: Johnny Dodds

Guitar: Lonnie Johnson

Piano: Lil Hardin

Banjo: Johnny St Cyr

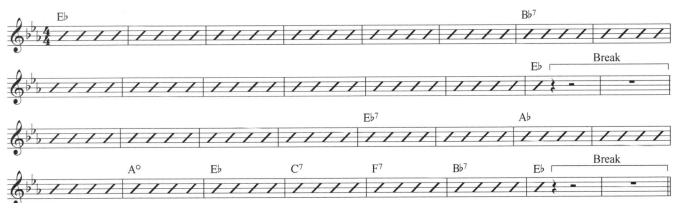

Each half of the chorus ends with a two-bar break, where the rhythm section stops dramatically for an unaccompanied solo. This becomes an important structural device. At the halfway point of a chorus it breaks up the solo effectively and creates a sudden change of texture; this offers an important point for the soloist to decorate between the two halves of his solo. Where the break occurs at the end of the chorus, the next musician can make a striking entrance before beginning their solo. The most effective use of the break is in the final chorus after the trombone solo, where Armstrong's ascending scale leads back to the final full ensemble.

| Introduction | 8 bars | 0'00" | Ensemble – New Orleans style |
|---|---|---|---|
| Chorus 1 | 32 bars | 0'09" | Trumpet solo (Louis Armstrong) |
| Chorus 2 | 32 bars | 0'45" | Clarinet solo (Johnny Dodds) |
| Chorus 3 | 32 bars | 1'21" | Vocal solo (Louis Armstrong) |
| Duet | 16 bars | 1'56" | Vocal + guitar (Lonnie Johnson) duet, no rhythm section |
| Link | 4 bars | 2'14" | Piano (Lil Hardin), a tempo |
| Chorus 4 | 16 bars | 2'18" | Trombone solo (Kid Ory) |
| | 16 bars | 2'36" | Full ensemble – New Orleans style |
| Coda | 4 bars | 2'51" | Vocal + guitar duet |

## Introduction

**New Orleans polyphony**

The introduction makes use of the final eight bars of the chorus' 32-bar chord pattern. The texture is typical of New Orleans polyphony:

➢ The short phrases of the trumpet melody are heard clearly

➢ The agile clarinet countermelody is balanced much further back in the mix, but is more audible in its higher register or in the rests between the trumpet phrases

➢ The trombone begins in traditional tailgate style, with glissandi up to sustained semibreves, before breaking into crotchets at the end of the introduction.

Early jazz bands sometimes played on the back of a truck. The trombonist would be at the back (by the tailgate) so there was plenty of room to use the slide, especially when playing a glissando.

## Chorus 1

The clarinet and trombone drop out, leaving the rhythm section to accompany the trumpet solo. Armstrong's solo is confident and well shaped. At the beginning of each of the first four phrases there is a two-note syncopated rhythm on the upbeat (see bars 0, 4, 8 and 12 in the example that follows). Armstrong's accent on the first note makes the syncopation a clear feature of the melody and gives it a strong sense of swing. The first full bar of each phrase is similar in rhythm (compare bars 1, 5, 9 and 13). The similarity of phrasing helps to make the improvisation highly melodic.

**Trumpet**

Most of the phrases extend over an octave, showing the soloist's agility and range. Note how the gradual ascent of the first notes of phrases contributes to energy in the melody: the solo begins on E♭ (bar 0 in the example), the second phrase on G (bar 4), the fourth phrase on A♭ (bar 12), and finally it reaches B♭ for the first note of the break. On the recording there is a 'rip' up to this B♭ note, which is like a very quick, subtle, glissando.

The second half of the solo breaks into a more varied and virtuosic pattern, with fewer rests between phrases; there are broken-chord figures and chromatic triplets. For the final phrase (bar 24) there is a sustained high G with a 'shake' (lip trill). This G anticipates the first note of the next phrase and provides an example of Armstrong's rhythmic freedom in his solos.

> In the example the printed notation follows the jazz convention of writing swung quavers as even notes.

## Chorus 2

The blues sound of Johnny Dodds' first note – which uses a clarinet 'smear' (jazz term for glissando) – makes a striking contrast with Armstrong. The solo begins in the high clarino (middle) and highest registers of the instrument. Dodds was known for his bright, assertive tone, which is even more piercing at these registers. The fast vibrato, which was fashionable in the 1920s, is most obvious at the end of long notes (known as 'terminal vibrato').

In the first few bars Dodds emphasises the strong crotchet beats of the bar, rather than using the syncopated upbeat of the trumpet solo. After a few bars he moves into swung quavers for the rest of the solo. The longer notes of the second break also make expressive use of a 'smear' (glissando) to add to the blues feel.

The accompaniment is in the banjo and piano only. Lil Hardin's energetic comping on the piano is not restricted to repeated chords. At the beginning of the chorus the bass octaves in the left hand are mostly alternating tonic and dominant, similar to the 'oom-pah' of the bass in a brass band. After a few bars the bass begins to move between registers. The right hands chords also move into a high register in places, which creates more variety in the texture.

## Chorus 3

The break at the end of Chorus 2 introduces Armstrong's singing for the first time. The piano drops out of the accompaniment, which leaves the banjo comping and Lonnie Johnson improvising countermelodies on the guitar.

**Scat**   The scat solos on some of the Hot Five recordings were very popular with the public. Armstrong is believed to have recalled that when he recorded *Heebie Jeebies* in 1926 he accidentally dropped the lyric sheet, forgot the words, and was forced to scat in order to complete the recording. Whatever the truth of this story, by the time of *Hotter Than That* in 1927 his scat choruses were a planned part of the composition. This technique was largely popularised by the Hot Five recordings.

A smear is a slide up to a note from below, and a fall off is a slide down at the end of a note.

Armstrong's vocal dexterity enables him to give the scat solos many of the same qualities as the earlier trumpet solo in Chorus 1. The first 16 bars have a similar overall shape, which includes the steady climb of the phrases moving towards the break. At this point Armstrong's glissando imitates a trumpet-style rip to a high B♭. Listen also for the regular use of smears, fall offs and vibrato. The use of smoother phrases in triplets exploits the melodic qualities of the singing voice, which contrast with the more instrumental rhythmic phrases used at the beginning of Chorus 3.

The second half is remarkable for its rhythmic organisation. Armstrong sings a succession of 24 dotted crotchets, which covers nine bars (see music example that follows). The polyrhythmic effect of dotted crotchets in the solo against the crotchet beat of the rhythm section creates a different pattern of syncopation in each bar. This was very unusual for its time and shows his gift for rhythmic freedom and invention.

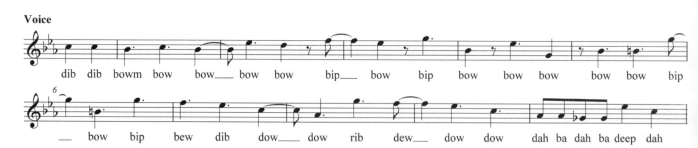

## Duet

Armstrong himself takes the break at the end of his Chorus 3, which extends it to a phrase of four bars (instead of the standard two bars). The rhythm section remains silent as voice and guitar exchange two-bar phrases in call and response style. Armstrong and Johnson give a strong blues flavour to their dialogue. At the beginning of each phrase notice the variation of smears and microtonal inflections on the 3rd degree of the scale (G or G♭). The different tunings of G are made a feature of the dialogue; this tonal device exploits the expressive flexibility of blues tuning, compared to the western classical approach to intonation.

# Chorus 4

After the interlude of the duet section, four bars of piano solo from Lil Hardin provide a **link** to the final chorus. Chorus 4 brings the music back to the original mood and tempo of the piece.

'Kid' Ory's trombone solo occupies the first half of the final chorus. He has four phrases of four bars each. Ory uses the slide on the trombone to decorate the pitches of the melody with three techniques: a glissando up to a note; a fall-off at the end of a note; a slide between notes. The rhythm section continues to drive forward an energetic accompaniment for the solo. In the background, Lil Hardin's piano decorates the harmony. Her style is typical of ragtime piano, with an elaborate countermelody in the right hand higher register.

The break at the end of the trombone solo brings Armstrong back to centre stage. Armstrong leads into the second half of Chorus 4 with an unaccompanied ascending scale in straight quavers, beginning as a chromatic scale and rising over an octave to a high B♭. The second half of the chorus begins in the **New Orleans polyphonic style**:

➢ The trumpet has repeated high B♭s in a syncopated rhythm for the first six bars, before breaking into the melody

➢ The clarinet plays an elaborate countermelody in a high register

➢ The trombone countermelody covers a wide range, providing some of the bass notes in the texture and some notes in the high register

➢ The rhythm section continues to comp.

The return of the full band at this point suggests a strong finale. Towards the end of Chorus 4 there is a dramatic sequence of 'stop time': the accompaniment plays short staccato chords separated by silences, which build up the anticipation for the end of the piece. The trumpet solo uses the syncopated dotted crotchet rhythms that had been used so effectively in the scat solo in Chorus 3.

In the closing bars of Chorus 4 Armstrong has one surprise left: he avoids the predictable full ensemble ending that the listener might expect. Instead Armstrong uses the final two-bar break at the end of Chorus 4 to return to the idea explored during the duet section: call and response with the guitar. The last guitar phrase reminds us of the blues style from the earlier dialogue. The final diminished chord makes for an intriguing and inconclusive ending.

**Further reading**

*Early Jazz* by Gunther Schuller. Oxford University Press, New York, 1986, ISBN 978-0-19-504043-2. Includes a significant chapter devoted to Louis Armstrong, with discussion and analysis of the structure of *Hotter Than That*.

*Louis Armstrong: An American Genius* by James Lincoln Collier. Oxford University Press, New York, 1985, ISBN 978-0-19-503727-2. A readable and informative biography, with much background information on the Hot Five period.

## Exercise 30

1. Explain why Louis Armstrong made such an impact on audiences and musicians. Use examples from *Hotter Than That* to illustrate your answer.

2. Why do you think Armstrong added a guitar player to the line up of the Hot Five in this recording? What effect does it have?

3. How does the rhythm section of this piece differ from that of Duke Ellington in *Koko*?

4. What is meant by New Orleans style collective improvisation?

# Duke Ellington: *Koko*

This is one of the three jazz recordings set for exams in June 2014.

Turn to page 144 for notes about exam questions on the jazz recordings.

*Koko*, recorded 6 March 1940 in Chicago for RCA Victor by Duke Ellington and His Famous Orchestra.

Alto saxophones: Johnny Hodges, Otto Hardwick

Clarinet: Barney Bigard

Tenor saxophone: Ben Webster

Baritone saxophone: Harry Carney

Trumpets: Wallace Jones, Cootie Williams, Rex Stewart

Trombones: Lawrence Brown, Joe 'Tricky Sam' Nanton, Juan Tizol

Guitar: Fred Guy

Piano: Duke Ellington

Double bass: Jimmy Blanton

Drums: Sonny Greer

Edward Kennedy 'Duke' Ellington (1899–1974) was brought up in Washington D.C. His musical middle-class parents arranged for him to be taught classical piano. However, the young Ellington preferred to learn the stride piano style of pianists such as James P. Johnson. With drummer Sonny Greer, Ellington formed his own band, the Washingtonians, and performed at the Kentucky Club in New York, toured dance venues and made his first recordings. It was at this time that he picked up the nickname 'Duke' – although some sources suggest that he acquired the name at an earlier time during his school years.

In the 1920s there was growing public demand for the new style of jazz known as swing. An important element in swing was the use of a much larger band (a big band or swing band) than in early jazz. The increase in size was because the music often accompanied dancing at venues of considerable size. The recording of *Koko* employs 15 players. The list of musicians for the *Koko* recording shows how the frontline soloists of New Orleans jazz had expanded into sections of trumpets, trombones and reeds (saxophones and clarinet).

Under the management of Irving Mills, Ellington's orchestra played in residency at the Cotton Club in Harlem between 1927 and 1931. The band performed for a wealthy white audience who enjoyed the vogue for exotic, African-style floorshows. Weekly radio broadcasts from the Cotton Club gave Ellington the type of public attention that few black bands had access to.

At the end of the Cotton Club residency Ellington's band toured Europe, where their music was already well known through their recordings. European critics were beginning to identify Ellington as the leading composer of jazz, comparing him favourably with classical composers. Returning to the United States the band toured extensively, and performed to both black and white audiences. Ellington composed many of his pieces while travelling on the train. Royalties from the sale of his songs made him one of the highest earning jazz musicians. Irving Mills' publicity encouraged the view of Ellington as an artist.

By 1940 Ellington's association with his manager Mills had ended; he had a new recording contract with the Victor label. Among the new musicians in the band were the saxophonist Ben Webster and a young bass player called Jimmy Blanton.

**The Ellington effect**

Although solos were usually improvised, collective improvisation by the entire band was impractical with such large numbers, and so musical arrangements became essential in the swing era. These were often in the form of notated parts for the players. The size of the band allowed the leader or arranger to choose from a wide range of sounds and textures:

➤ Chords arranged for sections of reeds, trumpets or trombones, with one player to each note

➤ Unison melodies or riffs for a section

➤ Antiphonal effects of pitting one section against another, either as call and response or as countermelodies

➤ Solo improvisation with accompaniment from one or more contrasting sections (for example, a trumpet solo accompanied by reeds) and the rhythm section.

Ellington's compositions and arrangements were strongly influenced by the qualities of the individuals in the band. Not only solos but also individual parts in the ensemble were tailored to the tone and preferred playing style of the players. Many of the band's numbers were developed over time during rehearsal; ideas and suggestions would be incorporated before being written down definitively. In this way the Ellington band developed a sound and style that was very personal to Ellington and his players. Billy Strayhorn, Ellington's arranger, called it 'the Ellington effect'.

Many of Ellington's players stayed with his band for many years. Players like Johnny Hodges, Cootie Williams and Ben Webster became well known to the public through their solos on Ellington's recordings.

Jimmy Blanton's double-bass playing created an immediate effect on the Ellington orchestra. He was only in the band for a few years (1939–1941) before he died of tuberculosis at the age of 23. His round, well-projected tone and sense of swing can be heard in recordings of this time, including his duets with Duke Ellington (for example *Mr J. B. Blues*). Ellington gave Blanton solos to play and made sure that he was always well recorded. In the choruses of *Koko* Blanton uses the walking bass style, while Sonny Greer keeps time on the hi-hat and Fred Guy comps on guitar. Apart from his solo, Ellington's piano playing is used very sparingly; in most of the choruses it comprises single staccato chords to highlight the first note of the 'x' motif.

Ellington recorded *Koko* again the following day after the 6 March recording. This alternative version is available on *Never No Lament: the Blanton-Webster Band* (RCA Bluebird 82876-50857-2), with interesting differences in the improvised solo parts.

**The rhythm section**

## Structure

The piece is made up of an introduction, seven choruses in 12-bar blues form, and a coda. The key is E♭ minor (minor tonality is unusual for a blues) with the use of D♭s and C♭s, which give a feeling of the aeolian mode.

| Introduction | 8 bars | 0'00" | |
|---|---|---|---|
| Chorus 1 | 12 bars | 0'12" | Valve trombone solo (Juan Tizol) |
| Chorus 2 | 12 bars | 0'32" | Trombone solo (Joe 'Tricky Sam' Nanton) |
| Chorus 3 | 12 bars | 0'51" | |
| Chorus 4 | 12 bars | 1'08" | Piano solo (Duke Ellington) |
| Chorus 5 | 12 bars | 1'26" | 3 trumpets in unison |
| Chorus 6 | 12 bars | 1'44" | Double bass solo (Jimmy Blanton) + ensemble |
| Chorus 7 | 12 bars | 2'03" | Full ensemble |
| Coda | 12 bars | 2'22" | |

The 12-bar blues pattern follows a standard chord progression, albeit in a minor key:

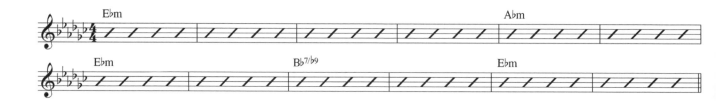

In *Koko* the music builds up gradually over the seven chorus repetitions of the blues. Ellington shows considerable control as he creates a sense of gathering momentum, using the four-note ostinato figure of the opening to create a sense of unity.

## Introduction

The opening bars of *Koko* set the brooding, jungle mood from the outset. In addition to the minor key, the dark sound of the baritone saxophone plays a low tonic pedal on E♭. The brighter sounds of trumpets and higher reeds are not used in the introduction. The hollow sounds of the tom-tom and the crotchet beat of the bass drum add to the distinctive African colour of this passage. The four-note rhythm 'x' motif (as named by Ken Rattenbury, English jazz trumpeter and author on Duke Ellington) is stated here for the first time (see example that follows). The syncopated chords in the three trombones move in parallel, descending chromatically in each phrase.

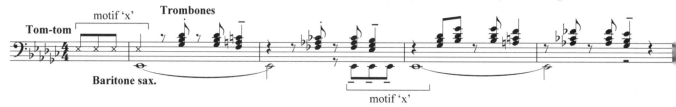

## Chorus 1

Juan Tizol plays the opening melody on a valve trombone (shifts in position would make it impossible to manage smoothly on a slide trombone). The example that follows shows how the rhythm of the 'x' motif is used for the first four notes.

The trombone phrases are answered by close harmonies in the four saxophones, which move in parallel. In the example that follows, note the rich sounds of 7th chords and the bluesy sound of having D♭ and D♮ in the same chord (marked with an asterisk).

The double bass is playing a pizzicato walking bass, filling in the notes of the chords in stepwise motion. The drums have changed from the jungle colouring to keeping time on the hi-hat and bass drum.

The repeated two-bar phrasing between the trombone and saxophones is shortened in bars 9 and 10 to two one-bar phrases. At this point the piano adds a syncopated octave B♭ (a dominant pedal) with a crescendo, which adds momentum towards the next chorus.

## Choruses 2 and 3

Joe Nanton has a double chorus for his trombone solo. His distinctive sound incorporates three effects. Firstly, he uses the growling 'ya-ya' sound for which he was well known. This sound is created using the plunger mute; it was common for all of Ellington's brass players. Secondly, Nanton uses a pixie (or straight) mute, which is fixed inside the trombone to create a buzz to the sound. Finally, his way of blowing contributed to the impression of words being pronounced. Nanton did his best to keep his methods secret in order to preserve his signature sound for himself.

Nanton's solo begins by emphasising the B♭, which Ellington had been repeating at the close of Chorus 1. He uses only a few pitches, but the vocalised sound with added smears and fall-offs creates a highly expressive calling effect that suits the jungle atmosphere of the piece. Nanton is accompanied by almost the full band:

1.  The four saxophones (without clarinet) are playing in a two-bar riff in a low unison, using the 'x' motif and sustained notes. The same riff is used in both choruses. Single staccato chords on the piano mark the first note of the 'x' rhythm.

2.  Three brass players (two trumpets and a trombone) play a syncopated rhythm, alternating repeated notes quickly between closed and open plunger mute positions. This is known as the 'du wah' effect because of the sound it makes. In notation the composer or arranger would write '+' over the note to indicate the mute and 'o' to create an open sound.

3.  The rhythm section keeps time; it is led by Jimmy Blanton's very clearly recorded walking bass, with the guitar comping and the drums keeping time.

The second half of the solo (Chorus 3) begins with higher pitches: the plunger mute is tight against the bell of the instrument, which restricts the sound further. Nanton then returns to the ya-ya style of playing to conclude the end of his solo.

## Chorus 4

For Duke Ellington's piano solo the accompanying riffs begin to move in one-bar phrases. The aeolian mode is reinforced by the repeated D♭s (the 7th of the E♭ minor chord) on each first beat.

The boldest harmony is in the dissonant piano solo. The right hand plays a whole-tone chord of F♭ – G♭ – B♭ – C, followed closely by a whole tone scale in semiquavers (ascending and descending over an octave and a half). The use of the bright high register of the piano emphasises its polytonal dissonance as it clashes with the E♭ minor chord in the rest of the band (and the left hand of the piano).

Four bars later, a whole-tone scale starting on C♭ (listen out for the F♮ and G♮ in the scale) creates a similar colourful dissonance against the A♭ minor chord. The solo ends with a syncopated E♭m⁷ chord. Ellington arranges this chord so that it leaps in pairs that are a 10th apart across the range of the instrument (for example, playing E♭ with a G♭ that is an octave and a 3rd higher).

## Chorus 5

The riff moves to the trumpets for the first time in Chorus 5, and reverts back to two-bar phrases. The repeated phrase is higher so that the 9th of the chord is the most prominent; it is more dissonant than the 7th in the previous chorus.

The sound of the unison trumpets with plunger mutes half open gives the music a more insistent feel. Apart from the piano, the whole ensemble is playing for Chorus 5. The reeds and trombones play a two-note rhythm and sustained chords, which answer each other antiphonally. The clarinet takes the highest note in the chord. The baritone sax has its own decorated figure.

## Chorus 6

The music in *Koko* has built up consistently so far. In Chorus 6, the 'x' motif is now harmonised by each section in turn. The example below shows how each section enters in imitation at a distance of one minim apart. The full band sustains the chord until an emphatic stop on two *fortissimo* repeated quavers.

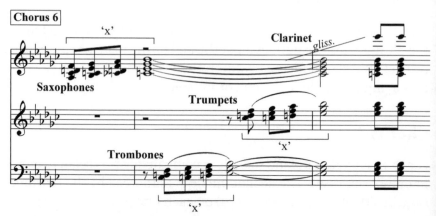

The double bass breaks the dramatic pause with a two-bar solo, which comprises a descending scale in walking bass crotchets. The rest of the chorus continues to alternate between the full band in imitation and solo bass in two-bar phrases. This type of chorus is often referred to as a 'chase chorus'.

## Chorus 7

The full ensemble takes over for the final climactic chorus, known as a 'shout chorus'. The melody is in unison saxophones. The clarinet supplies the highest note of the sustained chords in the brass section. Note the highly dissonant chords in this chorus. The E♭ minor chord at the beginning now includes a 7th, 9th and an 11th. Note also the insistent E♮s in the saxophones in bar 9 of the example: this causes a dissonance of a tritone (augmented 4th) against the B♭ in the bass. The phrase also includes whole-tone inflections, which Ellington had referred to earlier in his piano solo.

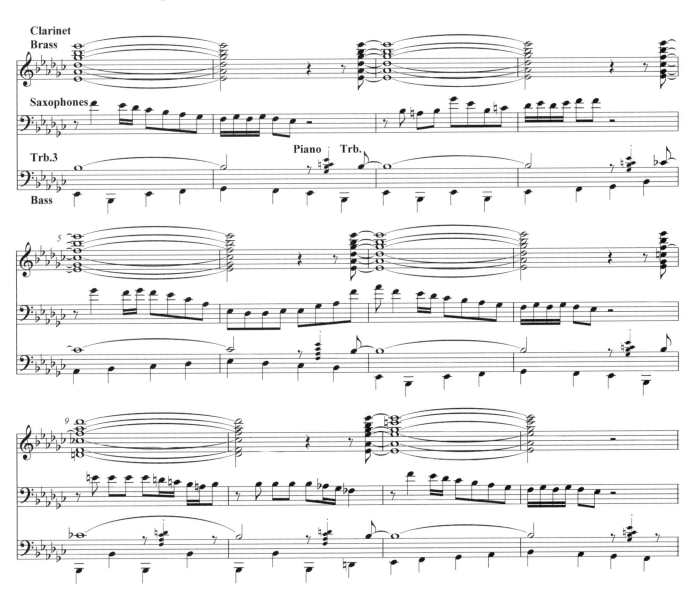

**Further reading**

*Duke Ellington, Jazz Composer* by Ken Rattenbury. Yale University Press, 1990, ISBN 978-0-300055-07-8. Includes a detailed discussion of Ellington's style and a full score and analysis of *Koko*.

*The Duke Ellington Reader* edited by Mark Tucker. Oxford University Press, New York, 1993, ISBN 978-0-195093-91-9. A collection of writings about Duke Ellington, which comprise reviews and articles from his contemporaries. Also includes Richard Boyer's article *The Hot Bach* (1944), which gives a good insight into Ellington's life on the road and his reputation at the time in the United States and abroad.

## Coda

The coda concludes *Koko* with a return to material from the introduction. This time, however, the orchestration is reduced to baritone sax, trombones and rhythm section. The final bars bring the whole band in, section by section, in ascending phrases. At this point 'straight eights' replace the swung rhythm (which had been a characteristic of the piece) to bring the music to a close.

### Exercise 31

1. What is meant by the jungle style?

2. Why do you think the big bands became popular in the 1930s and 1940s?

3. Explain the meaning of the following terms:

   a.  Walking bass

   b.  Shout chorus

   c.  Straight eights.

4. Describe how Ellington uses harmony and tonality in *Koko*.

5. Ellington's ability to create a sound that was unique to his band is often referred to as 'the Ellington Effect'. Give examples of how Ellington employs his signature sounds in this arrangement of *Koko*.

### Miles Davis: *Boplicity*

This is one of the three jazz recordings set for exams in June 2014.

Turn to page 144 for notes about exam questions on the jazz recordings.

Miles Davis (1926–1991) came to New York in 1944 as a teenager to study at the Julliard School of Music. He dropped out of college quickly to follow his idol Charlie Parker. By the age of 19 he was playing trumpet in Parker's quintet and making his first recordings.

The bebop style of Parker and trumpeter Dizzy Gillespie was fast and virtuosic. Although it was possible to dance to bebop, audiences tended not to. Bebop's hard-driven pace, dissonant harmonies and lack of easy melodies made it music for listening to rather than for dancing. Parker and his circle were happy to enjoy the intellectual status of being artists instead of entertainers. They discussed ideas about jazz music, such as how to construct new scales or chords. The group also took an interest in developments in classical music: Stravinsky, Ravel, Bartók and Prokofiev were favourite composers. The centre of much of these discussions was at the New York home of Canadian arranger Gil Evans.

By 1948 Miles Davis was breaking away from Parker and beginning to form his own groups. He was dissatisfied with bebop as a style. Davis avoided the fast-paced virtuosity that had been typical of Parker and Gillespie, and developed his own distinctive trumpet style:

➤ A quiet, understated sound, using the middle register, with very little vibrato

➤ Pitch bends at the beginning and ends of notes, and a wide variety of notes

➤ An economical style, avoiding double time and using silence

➤ A flexible sense of timing, anticipating and delaying notes against the underlying pulse.

## Gil Evans

Gil Evans was the arranger for the Claude Thornhill band. At the end of World War II the big bands were struggling. Although the Ellington and Basie bands continued to be successful, the public appetite for big band swing was diminishing. Whereas bands had once toured the country between week-long engagements, now even Duke Ellington's band played mostly one-night stands. For the record companies, singers were likely to sell better than instrumental jazz.

Thornhill worked hard to keep his band going. He adapted classical pieces for the swing band idiom, and developed a distinctive sound that became the basis of Gil Evans' arranging style:

➤ Unusual instrumentation, including the use of French horn and tuba

➤ Minimal use of vibrato

➤ Emphasis on soft, subdued sounds in low registers.

Most swing bands used sections of brass and reeds as contrasting groups. The antiphonal effect of contrasting sounds was important in band arrangements, such as in Duke Ellington's *Koko* (see pages 116–122). But Ellington's virtuoso band was also noted for its subtle arrangements and unusual combinations of instrumental timbres; features that both Davis and Evans admired. Gil Evans' technique of arranging extended the Ellington approach. The soft vibrato-less tone in the Thornhill band allowed Evans to blend the sounds of instruments from different sections of the band, and to create richly textured chords and subtle effects of instrumental colour.

## Birth of the Cool

*Boplicity* was one of 12 tracks recorded by Miles Davis and his Nonet in three sessions for Capitol Records in 1949–50. The recordings were released in pairs: one on each side of a standard three-minute disc, playing at 78 rpm. When *Boplicity* was reissued in 1957 it was in LP (long playing) format, a single album of 11 tracks, playing at 33 rpm. For this release the album's title was *Birth of the Cool*.

The *Birth of the Cool* recordings grew out of the discussions and active collaboration of the group gathered around Gil Evans. Many of the musicians involved were arrangers themselves, notably Gerry Mulligan (who is credited with three numbers). *Boplicity* (also known as 'Be Bop Lives') is credited for business reasons to Davis' mother, Cleo Henry, but the melody and arrangement are by Davis and Evans.

The nonet formation – nine players, comprising six horns (wind/brass instruments) and the standard rhythm section of piano, bass and drums – was considered by the group to be the ideal. At a time when bands featured a large group of saxophones, it was unusual to have only two. The French horn is used to blend the sound of the brass and saxophones. The tuba adds depth to the ensemble. Tuba player Bill Barber from the Thornhill band played in all of the *Birth of the Cool* recordings (as did saxophonists Mulligan and Lee Konitz).

Miles Davis was very much the leader of the band. His understated, coolly expressive approach set the tone for the other soloists. He arranged the recording contract with Capitol and booked a few engagements. The band's fresh approach drew interest from musicians and critics, but the public remained largely indifferent.

By the 1957 release Miles Davis was an established and marketable star. During the early 1950s the trend towards a softer, less dauntingly complex style of jazz became known as 'cool jazz'. Some of the nonet's musicians were key figures in the development of this style, notably Lee Konitz, Gerry Mulligan and John Lewis. The rebranding of the recordings as *Birth of the Cool* was a recognition of the influence and importance of these sessions.

*Boplicity*, recorded 22 April 1949 in New York for Capitol Records by Miles Davis and His Orchestra.

Trumpet: Miles Davis

Trombones: J.J. Johnson

French horn: Sandy Siegelstein

Tuba: John 'Bill' Barber

Alto saxophone: Lee Konitz

Baritone saxophone: Gerry Mulligan

Piano: John Lewis

Double bass: Nelson Boyd

Drums: Kenny Clarke

## Structure

*Boplicity* is based on a standard 32-bar song form. The moderate tempo meant that it could only be played three times within the three-minute limit of a 78 rpm disc.

| Chorus 1 | 32 bars | 0'00" | A (8 bars) | Full ensemble (no piano) |
|---|---|---|---|---|
| | | | A (8 bars) | |
| | | | B (8 bars) | |
| | | | A (8 bars) | |
| Chorus 2 | 34 bars | 0'57" | A (8 bars) | Baritone saxophone solo (Gerry Mulligan) |
| | | | A (8 bars) | |
| | | 1'25" | B (6 bars) | Full ensemble (no piano) |
| | | | +4 bars | Trumpet solo (Miles Davis) |
| | | | A (8 bars) | Full ensemble (no piano) |

| Chorus 3 | 32 bars + 1 bar | 1'57" | A (8 bars) | Trumpet solo with ensemble |
| --- | --- | --- | --- | --- |
| | | | A (8 bars) | Trumpet solo with rhythm section |
| | | 2'25" | B (8 bars) | Piano solo (John Lewis) |
| | | | A (9 bars) | Full ensemble (no piano) |

Despite the AABA form, *Boplicity* is not easy to follow when listening to the recording. A number of features disguise the shape of the choruses:

➤ The bridge in Chorus 2 is extended to ten bars (six bars of full ensemble followed by four bars of trumpet solo)

➤ The trumpet solo begins during the B section of Chorus 2 and then continues through to the next B section of Chorus 3; therefore, there is no change of soloist for the next chorus (Chorus 3)

➤ The consistent use of the frontline players to accompany the trumpet makes the start of Chorus 3 less obvious

➤ The accompaniment is fully written out, making the piece sound through-composed. Evans avoids the riff-based style that Ellington uses to mark his choruses

➤ The subtle harmonies of the opening A sections are not replicated in Choruses 2 and 3; each chorus has its own chord structure.

The rhythm section features the double bass playing a pizzicato walking bass. The drums are played with brushes throughout the piece. The piano is mostly silent during full ensemble passages, where the already richly scored textures do not need any additional chordal support from the piano.

## Chorus 1

*Boplicity* has no introduction. The opening chorus is fully written out for the full ensemble, minus the piano. The melody on the trumpet is doubled an octave lower by the baritone saxophone. The six horns (wind/brass) form a rhythmic unit that plays complex chords in close harmony. The following example is the opening eight bars (section A) of Chorus 1.

The F major tonality is not immediately apparent. Evans begins with a Gm7 chord and uses chromatic chords; each F chord uses different extensions (7ths, 9ths, 11ths). Only in bars 6–7 does a dominant pedal of C suggest the key more clearly. Even the final chord has the rich sound of an 11th chord, with the G and B♭ sharpened to G♯ and B♮. (Try playing F major and E major triads at the same time to get the same effect.)

The first four bars are highly syncopated. The melody notes rarely coincide with the strong beat in double bass and drums. The triplet in bar 2 adds to the rhythmic flexibility of the melody. By contrast the answering phrase (bars 5–8) hits the strong beats regularly. There is a repeated ascending 3rd figure (marked 'b' in the Chorus 1 example) over the syncopated dominant pedal in the tuba and the clear offbeat hits of the cymbal. After the ambiguities of the opening, the second half of section A helps to provide the certainty of a completed phrase.

The B section has more conventional phrasing and chord progressions. The melody uses the six-note tag from the end of the trumpet's first phrase (bar 4, marked 'a' in the Chorus 1 example). The repetition of the 'a' motif gives this section a clear shape.

## Chorus 2

**Baritone sax solo**

The baritone saxophone is not a commonly used solo instrument. Gerry Mulligan was one of its most important exponents, with a number of his solos featured on the *Birth of the Cool* recordings. Mulligan is an important figure in the development of 'cool jazz'. This style is often associated with the West Coast of the United States, where Mulligan was based in the 1950s. He formed a successful quartet with trumpeter Chet Baker in Los Angeles. In 1960 he formed a 13-piece band, recording the album *Concert Jazz Band*.

Mulligan's light, soft tone is typical of cool jazz. He plays in the middle and upper registers, using little vibrato.

His solo is clear and uncomplicated. Mulligan uses a relaxed crotchet and swung quaver movement, and avoids the complex double time of many bebop solos. The melody develops in a logical, unhurried way. He uses silences to create a feeling of space, and each phrase seems to develop organically from the initial idea. For example the melody in the second half of the solo (bars 9–16 in the next example) grows out of the four-note ascending figure that starts at bar $9^4$, with pairs of ascending quavers (marked 'c') repeated higher as the melody ascends.

The accompaniment is for the rhythm section only. The chord pattern is a simpler version of the opening chorus.

At the bridge (section B of Chorus 2) the other frontline instruments enter in quiet low octaves, the C minor tonality darkening the mood. The brighter sound of the trumpet is left out. The frontline melody (still in octaves) climbs quickly to a high F then descends slowly in a sequence of syncopated phrases to a sustained F, two octaves below. The extended descent lengthens this part of the bridge section by two bars (i.e. six bars in total).

The trumpet solo begins to the accompaniment of sustained chords in the rest of the ensemble; the bass plays repeated B♭s. After the band's mysterious and meandering descent to the low F during the six preceding bars of section B, the bright sound of the trumpet then transforms the mood. The first four bars of the example that follows are the trumpet solo in B, bringing the return of a regular quaver movement to the melody. There is a clear sense of direction in the modulation through the circle of 5ths and in the way the trumpet melody is shaped. The melody gradually reaches higher and higher until it reaches a top F (bar 4[4] in the example) – two octaves above the band's low F from four bars earlier.

**Trumpet solo**

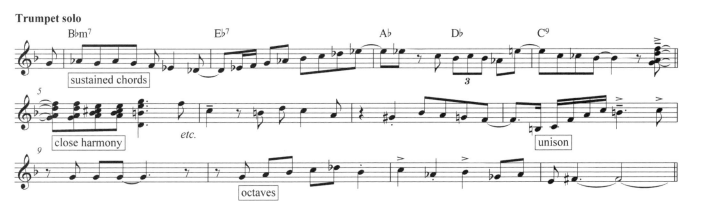

In the 28 bars led by the trumpet (between Chorus 2 and 3) the role of the accompaniment changes several times; this creates a subtle interplay between Davis and the band. The table below traces the development:

| | Trumpet | Other frontline | Rhythm section |
|---|---|---|---|
| **End of Chorus 2** | | | |
| 4 bars | Solo melody (notated in trumpet example above) gradually ascends to F | Sustained chords Syncopated chord changes to match ascent of trumpet solo Crescendo | Piano, bass and drums Repeated crotchets in bass: $B\flat m^7 - E\flat^7 - A\flat - D\flat - C^9$ |
| 4 bars | Melody part | Full group at climax of trumpet melody Chordal/homophonic; follows rhythm of the melody | Piano drops out Bass and drums only Bass resumes walking pattern |
| 4 bars | Melody | Trumpet, saxophones, trombone in octaves Horn drops out Tuba plays bass Tremolo in baritone sax and tuba on final sustained chord | Bass and drums |
| **Beginning of Chorus 3** | | | |
| 8 bars | Improvised solo A bar of double time | Chords, antiphonal Crushed note (acciaccatura) and falling 3rd figure Fall-off on last chord | Piano, bass and drums Detached chords in piano |
| 8 bars | Improvised solo Use of silences/rests | No other frontline players | Rhythm section only |

## Chorus 3

The table above covers Section A of Chorus 3 (and the trumpet solo). At Section B, the bridge, the texture is reduced to that of a jazz piano trio. John Lewis' eight-bar piano solo continues the consistent pattern of the solos so far; he uses a relaxed swung quaver movement and a long silence between the phrases. The first four bars of his melody emphasise the interval of a perfect 5th (B♭ to F). This figure is briefly echoed two octaves lower in the B to F♯ that starts the second four-bar phrase of Section B.

The piece ends with a full-band reprise of the final A section. There is no coda. Instead, this version of the A section is one bar longer than usual. The ascending 3rd figure over the dominant pedal (referred to as 'b' in the music example on page 126) is now played twice more to extend the melody to a suitable conclusion. The additional syncopated accents in drums and cymbals give the final section an extra sense of swing. The quiet and contained mood continues to the end.

The final three chords – fully scored, but *piano* – repeat the opening three chords of *Boplicity*; they are played in augmentation (longer, sustained notes) with the trumpet ending on a D (6th degree in F major) instead of a C. The drums have a quiet fill on the final chord. The tuba plays a tremolo between two notes before coming to rest on its sonorous low F.

## Exercise 32

1. What is cool jazz? How is it different from bebop?

2. Why do you think *Boplicity* interested musicians and critics more than the public when it was first released?

3. Compare the arranging techniques of Duke Ellington and Gil Evans.

4. List the similarities and differences between the trumpet styles of Louis Armstrong and Miles Davis.

5. How did the life of a jazz musician change between the 1920s and the end of the 1940s?

**Further reading**

*Miles Davis – Birth of the Cool: scores from the original parts* (including *Boplicity*). Published by Hal Leonard, ISBN 978-0-634-00682-1.

*Miles Davis: The Definitive Biography* by Ian Carr. Harper Collins, 1982/1999, ISBN 978-0-006530-26-8. An absorbing account of Davis' life and music, including his classic album *A Kind of Blue*, his collaborations with Gil Evans and his later experiments with jazz-rock fusion.

*It's About That Time: Miles Davis On and Off Record* by Richard Cook. Atlantic Books, 2005, ISBN 978-1-84354-332-9. An insightful guide to Davis' many recorded albums.

*Gil Evans: Out of the Cool – his life and music* by Stephanie Stein Crease. A Cappella Books, Chicago, 2002, ISBN 978-1-55652493-6. A readable and appreciative account of Gil Evans and his achievements.

# New Orleans Rhythm Kings: *Tin Roof Blues*

This is one of the three jazz recordings set for the exams in June 2015 and June 2016. Turn to page 144 for notes about exam questions on the jazz recordings.

*Tin Roof Blues*, recorded 13 March 1923 for Gennett Records in Richmond, Indiana, by the New Orleans Rhythm Kings.

| | |
|---|---|
| Trumpet: | Trumpet: Paul Mares |
| Trombone: | George Brunies |
| Clarinet: | Leon Roppolo |
| Piano: | Mel Stitzel |
| Drums: | Ben Pollack (although not audible on this track) |

## New Orleans jazz

In the very early 20th century, New Orleans was the scene of a melting-pot of musical styles which gave birth to jazz. Marching band music such as that of John Philip Sousa, ragtime, blues and popular dances such as the quadrille, combined within a thriving and ethnically mixed artistic community. There was high demand for live music in New Orleans, and musicians keen to provide fresh, marketable material were adventurous in mixing elements of different styles. The resulting style, which became known as Dixieland jazz, was characterised by the following:

➤ A '**front line**' comprising trumpet or cornet, clarinet and trombone. Usually the trumpet would take the main melody, with the clarinet harmonising above (in a manner similar to that of the piccolo in marching band music), and the trombone playing lower harmonies.

➤ A **rhythm section** comprising piano, drums, a banjo and a bass line. The bass line was originally played by a tuba or sousaphone, but later the upright (double) bass took over this role. The guitar replaced the banjo as time went on. The drums often played a simple rhythm with the bass drum on the first and third beats of the bar, and the snare on the second and fourth beats: this is identical to the pattern most commonly used in marching band music. The piano and banjo often played repeated chords, a technique known as **comping**.

➤ Syncopated rhythms: these were derived from ragtime, where 'ragging' referred to the act of taking a melody and varying it by syncopating its rhythm. This idea, together with **polyrhythm** (playing different rhythms at the same time) can be traced back to African music.

➤ **Collective improvisation**, where the 'front line' instruments improvise at the same time.

➤ **Twelve bar blues** was used frequently as a structural and harmonic framework.

➤ The decoration of melody lines with '**blue**' **notes** – those which are outside the notes of the key of the music, or which are 'bent' to fall 'in the cracks' between the pitches of conventional scales.

## The New Orleans Rhythm Kings

In the early 1920s there was a migration of musicians from New Orleans to Chicago, and this is what brought about the formation of the New Orleans Rhythm Kings, often referred to as NORK. The promise of better paid work and a buzzing scene with plenty of good musicians led the trumpeter Paul Mares and trombonist George Brunies to leave New Orleans and head for Chicago. Work for jazz musicians in Chicago at this time was to be found in nightclubs and on riverboats. Chicago was also at the centre of the new craze for radio, which gave impetus to the development of the popularity of jazz, as well as presenting opportunities for musicians to become well known. Mares and Brunies found work at a club called the Friar's Inn, and in 1921-22 performed in a band known as the Friar's Society Orchestra. Here they attracted a lot of attention from interested musicians, and recorded a series of records under the name New Orleans Rhythm Kings for Gennett Records in 1922-23 which became very well-known.

## Tin Roof Blues

Three takes of *Tin Roof Blues* were recorded, the one set for the AS exam being the second. At this time, recordings were made acoustically, with the whole band being recorded together and with no capacity for editing the resultant recording. The polished performance captured here suggests that NORK had played *Tin Roof Blues* frequently in their live performances. It is typical of New Orleans-style jazz in that there is a front line of trumpet, clarinet, and trombone, with the trumpet taking the lead melodies. Collective improvisations are also essential to the New Orleans sound, where all the frontline players improvise together around a chord pattern. This required a subtle etiquette where all players were sensitive to what everyone else was doing, with the individual lines weaving together and players being careful not to compete with each other.

The sound of the front line is characterised by fast, insistent vibrato in the clarinet. Leon Roppolo was regarded as a master of this style, and his solo on *Tin Roof Blues* is an excellent example of his virtuosity: in fact, the three takes of the song demonstrate three very different, breathtaking clarinet solos. The other characteristic sound of NORK, and of New Orleans jazz in general, is the **trombone glissando**, or **tailgate**. Legend has it that this nickname came from the tradition of New Orleans bands playing in the back of a truck to publicise their clubs, and a lack of space leading to the trombonist having to hang his instrument out of the back (or tailgate) of the truck. Added to the front line was a rhythm section of piano, (and occasionally drums – although not on *Tin Roof Blues*). There is no bass other than that provided by the left hand of the piano.

## Structure

*Tin Roof Blues* is based on the 12-bar blues chord sequence beloved of New Orleans jazz and many other styles since. The basic structure of each chorus involves three lines of four bars each:

| I | I | I | I |
|:---:|:---:|:---:|:---:|
| B♭ | B♭ | B♭ | B♭ |
| IV | IV | I | I |
| E♭ | E♭ | B♭ | B♭ |
| V | IV | I | I |
| F | E♭ | B♭ | B♭ |

Although the 12-bar blues is based on primary triads (I, IV and V), these chords are not used in the type of functional, key-defining way found in the Baroque and Classical scores you have studied. This is largely the result of adding **blue notes** – particularly the flattened 3rd and 7th degrees of the scale.

The overall structure is this:

| | | | |
|---|---|---|---|
| Intro | 4 bars | 0:00-0:08 | Piano |
| Chorus 1 *Tin Roof Blues* | 12 bars | 0:08-0:37 | Ensemble, with trumpet taking the lead with a composed melody: collective improvisation from clarinet and trombone |
| Chorus 2 Derived from *Jazzin' Babies Blues* | 12 bars | 0:37-1:05 | More chordal approach with frontline instruments playing in harmony |
| Chorus 3 Derived from *Jazzin' Babies Blues* | 12 bars | 1:05-1:32 | More structured approach with frontline instruments playing in harmony |
| Chorus 4 | 12 bars | 1:32-1:59 | Trombone solo |
| Chorus 5 | 12 bars | 1:59-2:25 | Clarinet solo |
| Chorus 6 | 12 bars | 2:25-2:52 | Collective improvisation from front line: much freer than Chorus 1, with trumpet improvising |
| Outro | 2 bars | 2:52 | Ensemble, led by trumpet |

**The ensemble choruses** The texture heard here, with the trumpet on the main melody, the clarinet above and the trombone below, was the standard organisation for **collective improvisation** in the New Orleans style, and is sometimes referred to as **New Orleans polyphony**.

Harmonically, *Tin Roof Blues* demonstrates many classic features of early jazz. As soon as the first chorus starts, chord I features an added minor 7th, and so is B♭⁷. Here, the trumpet takes the principal melody of the song. Nearly every recording is instrumental, but the published lyrics, by Walter Melrose, are:

The second and third ensemble choruses feature a descending chromatic figure, with the clarinet a 6th above the trumpet, and the trombone a 6th below:

This distinctive melody or 'strain' is shared with *Jazzin' Babies Blues*, recorded by many New Orleans artists in the 1920s including Joe 'King' Oliver. Intriguingly, this melody was also known by various other titles, including *Pee Hole Blues* and *Don't Get Funky 'Cause Your Water's On*.

The final chorus features much freer improvisation, with Paul Mares freeing himself from a composed melody to join in. Because three takes of *Tin Roof Blues* were recorded on the same day, it is possible to compare the performances and see the extent of the players' inventiveness in their improvisations. It becomes immediately apparent that clarinettist Leon Roppolo, in particular, applied great skill and imagination to his improvisation, with each take being significantly different from the others.

There are many examples of **blue notes** – notes which do not belong to the Bb scale – most particularly in the clarinet part. Leon Roppolo's fills at the end of each line feature slides and inflections of pitch which defy conventional notation, and are most certainly 'blue'. The conflict between major and minor, shown in the inclusion of the minor and major 3rds on each chord of the sequence, together with slides which encompass notes in between, are at the very heart of what makes the blues work, musically and emotionally.

At the end of the ensemble choruses we hear some dissonance which at first might sound like a mistake. However, it is repeated, so we must assume that it is intentional. It involves a series of parallel minor 9ths between the trumpet and clarinet:

There is much more to this figure than just a return to a simple tonic chord.

Rhythmically, the whole piece is characterised by **swing rhythms**, where pairs of quavers are not played 'straight', but have a lazy, almost triplet feel:

The degree to which a rhythm is swung is not exact, so the notation above should not be taken as an indication that the first quaver will always be exactly twice the length of the second. However, a piece written in $\frac{4}{4}$ sounds much more like it is in $\frac{12}{8}$. The piano and clarinet, in particular, play many triplets, which reinforce this feel:

The piano style features even crotchets in the left hand throughout *Tin Roof Blues*, with much syncopation in the right hand. If you compare the piano introduction above with a typical passage from a Scott Joplin rag (below), you can see immediately the similarities and differences.

Scott Joplin *Maple Leaf Rag*

**Tempo di marcia**

Stitzel's left hand patterns in *Tin Roof Blues* are less rigid than those in the rag piece: sometimes they have a bass-chord-bass-chord pattern, and sometimes a bass-chord-chord-bass pattern, or, later in the song, held 5-beat chords or simple repeated crotchet chords. With the absence of a separate bass part, and a lack of audible drums on the recording, the piano forms the rhythm section all by itself. So, the simple crotchets of the left hand have not only a historical basis but also fulfil the necessary function of underpinning both the rhythm and the harmony. Stitzel's playing on this recording represents the bridge between ragtime piano style and the East Coast stride pianists of the later 1920s and 1930s. Stride pianists, such as Fats Waller, employed a very similar figuration, but with wider leaps between the bass and chords in the left hand, and an even greater emphasis on improvisation.

**The solo choruses**

George Brunies' trombone solo is surprisingly staid: it returns repeatedly to the root note of the chord, and only includes a couple of tailgates and the incorporation of 7ths and minor 3rds into the melody. The range of the trombone solo is a 13th:

Leon Roppolo's clarinet solo is much more full of interest. Notation cannot show every nuance of his style, which includes glissandi, **smears**, **fall offs** and **scoops** to bend the pitch. He starts with a whinnying sound on a high F, and there is barely a note that is attacked cleanly or played 'straight'. His highly legato style involves an incredibly supple approach to pitch, with almost every note being slid onto from above or below, emphasising the not-quite-major-or-minor approach to 3rds which encapsulates the spirit of blues. Any sustained notes are embellished with a strong vibrato that could almost be described as tremolo. The range of the clarinet solo is two octaves, and does not employ the low, chalumeau register of the instrument as many New Orleans clarinettists liked to:

> A **smear** is a slide up to a note from below, a **fall off** is a slide down at the end of a note, and a **scoop** is a slide down and back up again during the course of a note.

> The chalumeau register is the lowest octave on the clarinet, with a rich, dark sound. It is named after the instrument that was the predecessor of the clarinet.

Both solo choruses are accompanied by the piano, with Mel Stitzel continuing the figuration that has been present throughout the number.

**Further listening**

Try to listen to other recordings by the New Orleans Rhythm Kings, and compare them with those by the Original Dixieland Jazz Band and Joe 'King' Oliver.

### Exercise 33

1.  Which features of the New Orleans Rhythm Kings' style help to account for the popularity of their recordings?

2.  Name the American city from which many members of NORK came, and explain the importance of that city in the history of jazz.

3.  Explain the meaning of each of the following terms:

    i)   smear

    ii)  collective improvisation

    iii) swing rhythm

4.  Which two degrees of the scale are most likely to be altered when playing blue notes?

## Dizzy Gillespie: *Manteca*

The son of a local band leader, Dizzy Gillespie (1917-1993) was born in South Carolina and taught himself to play trumpet and trombone. He got his first job as a professional trumpeter in a jazz orchestra in 1935, and went on to play with some of the great jazz musicians of the day, including Ella Fitzgerald, Cab Calloway and Earl Hines. The bands that Gillespie played in at this time made their living through residencies at jazz clubs, series of concerts at major concert halls, radio broadcasts and recording contracts. In 1942, while still playing with Earl Hines' band, Gillespie wrote *A Night in Tunisia*, which was a taste of the groundbreaking contribution he was soon to make to the development of modern jazz styles, bebop and Afro-Cuban jazz. At the time, the predominant jazz form was swing, and Gillespie's music displayed very different ideas concerning rhythm and harmony.

This is one of the three jazz recordings set for the exams in June 2015 and June 2016. Turn to page 144 for notes about exam questions on the jazz recordings.

To get an idea of what popular jazz of the late 1930s and early 1940s sounded like, and just how different Gillespie's music was, compare *A Night in Tunisia* with *Take the 'A' Train* by Duke Ellington's orchestra and *Jumpin' at the Woodside* by Count Basie.

In 'Latin' music, the rhythm relies on equal quavers rather than the unequal, 'swung' quavers that had become standard in jazz. The predominance of drums in Latin music could be explained by the fact that slaves in Latin American countries were allowed to play drums, so the West African music of their background lived on in a way that was not possible in the United States, where such musical activity was not permitted.

*Manteca*, recorded 30 December 1947 in New York for RCA Victor.

Trumpet/vocal: Dizzy Gillespie

| | |
|---|---|
| Trumpet: | Benny Bailey, Dave Burns, Elmon Wright, Lammar Wright, Jr. |
| Trombone: | Ted Kelly, Bill Shepherd |
| Alto sax: | John Brown, Howard Johnson |
| Tenor sax: | 'Big Nick' Nicholas, Joe Gayles |
| Baritone sax: | Cecil Payne |
| Piano: | John Lewis |
| String bass: | Al McKibbon |
| Drums: | Kenny Clarke |
| Congas: | Chano Pozo |

The son clave (pronounced clah-veh) rhythm is one that underpins a huge proportion of Afro-Cuban music, even if, as here, any particular instrument does not play it explicitly. You will be familiar with this idea if you have studied salsa for OCR GCSE Music. The clave rhythm consists of a group of three notes (the tresillo) and a group of two notes, which can be played in either order as a '3:2' clave, or as a '2:3' clave. *Manteca* has a 2:3 clave:

From the mid 1940s he was one of a set of jazz musicians, including Charlie Parker and Thelonious Monk, who were at the forefront of the development of new jazz styles. With Charlie Parker, Gillespie developed the bebop style, which was based on swing rhythms. The United States' entry into World War II in 1941 absorbed huge human and economic resources, with the result that the big bands of swing got smaller. An emphasis on fast, virtuosic, improvised solos took the place of the pre-composed arrangements of big band swing. Bebop bands experimented with irregular phrasing and dissonant interpretations of standard chord changes.

While Gillespie was at the forefront of the development of bebop, he was also interested in Latin music (music from the Spanish-speaking countries of North and South America), particularly the rhythms, and wanted to incorporate some Latin ideas into his own music. In 1945, Mario Bauzá, a Latin jazz trumpeter working with Gillespie in New York, introduced him to conga player Chano Pozo, who became a great friend and was hired to play congas in his band, co-writing some of the numbers that represent the emergence of the Afro-Cuban jazz style. For a while, Gillespie referred to this new style as **Cu-bop**.

### Structure

*Manteca* was co-written by Dizzy Gillespie, Chano Pozo and Gil Fuller in 1947. Pozo composed the **guajeos** (Afro-Cuban ostinatos), Gillespie the two choruses, and Fuller the horn lines. The song is a fusion of a typical jazz 32-bar song form and ostinato-based Latin jazz. The use of a big band, and moments of swing rhythm feel, walking bass, and tuneful melodies in the choruses, are the jazz elements, which have more in common with 1940s swing than the emergent bebop style. The congas, the static harmony of the intro, interlude and a section, the mambo bell rhythm of the a section melody, and the underlying **son clave** rhythm are the Afro-Cuban elements.

| Intro | 28 bars | 0:00-0:38 | A slow build-up of texture, starting with Pozo's congas and a bass vamp. |
|---|---|---|---|
| Chorus 1 | 40 bars | 0:38-1:33 | Five 8-bar phrases: *a a b b¹ a* |
| Interlude | 10 bars | 1:33-1:47 | Similar to the intro |
| Chorus 2 | 40 bars | 1:47-2:42 | Five 8-bar phrases: *c c b b¹ a* |
| Outro | 16 bars | 2:42 | A reverse of the intro, with the layers of vamps dying out |

### The introduction

| 22 bars static harmony: layers of vamps build up towards an exuberant Gillespie trumpet solo at 0:18 | 2 bars of chord changes | Texture dies down back to layered vamps: 4 bars |
|---|---|---|

The introduction consists of four separate, 2-bar ostinatos or **vamps**. Only three pitches are used: B♭, A♭ and F, and even Pozo's congas are tuned to these notes. The first vamp to be heard is from the congas, rapidly followed by the string bass. In turn, the baritone sax and trombone are added:

**Vamp** is used in jazz, and in music theatre scores where the term 'vamp 'til ready' is often seen, indicating that the player should repeat the ostinato until a cue on stage indicates that they should stop.

Note that all the quavers here are 'straight': the rhythmic interest in Latin music comes from the irregular accents, and here all four vamps display accents in different places, giving the music its distinctive kaleidoscopic feel.

Harmonically, the introduction is static: there is no concept of chord changes except in bars 23 and 24 (hear this at 0:29). This is typical of Afro-Cuban dance music, but did not become a common feature of jazz until the late 1950s. All of the As are A♭s, even though the music is in B♭ major: it is very common in jazz for the leading-note to be flattened, as is the case here. The prevailing chord is B♭$^7$, a minor 7th tonic chord (I$^7$).

**Ostinato**, **riff**, **vamp**, and **guajeo** are all words that mean roughly the same thing: they all refer to a repeating pattern (melodic or rhythmic) in the music. Ostinato is Italian for 'obstinate', and is a catch-all term for a repeating musical idea. The word 'riff' tends to be used when talking about rock, pop or jazz. 'Guajeo' specifically refers to an ostinato pattern in an Afro-Cuban piece.

## Chorus 1

| *a* | *a* | *b* | *b$^1$* | *a* |
|---|---|---|---|---|
| 6 bars of static harmony with sax/trumpet call and response: 2 bars of chord changes | Repeat of previous section: 6 + 2 bars | Chord changes throughout. Smooth saxes answered by brass. 8 bars | Chord changes throughout. Trumpet solo. 8 bars | Repeat of previous *a* section. 6 + 2 bars |

The *a* section consists of a simple, effective call and response between the saxophones and the brass. Because this starts with the same static harmony as the introduction, it enables the Latin style and the 32-bar song form to flow seamlessly. The rhythm of the melody in the *a* section uses a popular mambo bell rhythm from Cuban music:

In the *b* section (or **bridge**) the rhythmic feel switches to swing, with a walking bass rather than the repeating vamps that have been heard previously, and we are now well and truly in the territory of American, not Afro-Cuban, jazz, although Pozo keeps going with the same conga rhythm that he has been playing throughout. The first eight bars of this section are played by mellifluous saxes, answered by the brass, while *b¹* is a Gillespie solo. Gillespie later wrote that after the first eight bars of the bridge, he still had not resolved to B♭, so he had to add another eight bars, diverging from standard 32-bar form.

Dizzy Gillespie is regarded as one of the greatest jazz trumpeters ever to have lived, and it is said that his style and technique was almost impossible to copy, so aspiring trumpeters used other players as their model. The features of his playing are as follows:

➤ A range which could go right up into the 'screaming' register of the trumpet: in *Manteca* this reaches an F above a high C (E♭ concert pitch)

➤ Great agility, with the ability to cover a great many notes accurately over a wide range in a single phrase

➤ Variety of tone, from the 'screaming' high notes to a lush, romantic sound

➤ Use of many non-harmony notes, taking the melody line into adventurous harmonic territory but always resolving dissonances so that the sense of tonality is not lost

➤ Repeated notes played with great variety of articulation, tone and inflection.

**32-bar form**, or AABA form, became the standard pattern for popular songs in the United States in the mid-1920s. It subsequently became a standard structure in jazz, allowing more variety than 12-bar blues. The A section is known as the **refrain**, with the B section called the **middle 8** or **bridge**, and usually featuring a modulation. George Gershwin's *I Got Rhythm* is a well-known example of a song with this form.

### Interlude

The 10-bar interlude starts with bass and percussion, and is a compressed version of the introduction, building up rapidly to a 'shout' from the whole band which spills over into Chorus 2. The trombones now play the vamp previously played by the bass, and the bass now plays the trombone vamp. However, the rests that were previously featured in the trombone vamp are not present: this is for practical reasons, as the bass is needed to play continuously in order to play its part in the rhythm section and keep the music driving forward.

### Chorus 2

| *c* | *c* | *b* | *b¹* | *a* |
|---|---|---|---|---|
| Chord changes under tenor sax solo | Sax solo continues. Chord changes with walking bass | Chord changes throughout. Trumpet section answered by saxes | Chord changes throughout Trumpet solo | Repeat of a section from Chorus 1 |

Again, it is in the bridge that the swing elements of the piece shine through. 'Big Nick' Nicholas's tenor sax comes to the fore here, with the trumpet section adding feisty comments throughout the first *c* section. They take a rest during the second *c* section as the bass changes to a walking pattern and follows the same chord changes as Gershwin's *I Got Rhythm*:

**Further reading**

*To be, or Not... To Bop*, by Dizzy Gillespie and Al Fraser. University of Minnesota Press, 2009. ISBN 978-0816665471.

| I | vi⁷ | ii⁷ | V⁷ |
|---|---|---|---|
| B♭ | Gm⁷ | Cm⁷ | F⁷ |

Mischievously, Nicholas does not go along with this, and throws in a reference to Rodgers and Hart's 1934 song *Blue Moon*, which you can hear at 1:57.

---

## Exercise 34

1. Make a chart to show which features of *Manteca* belong to Afro-Cuban music, and which ones to swing. Give specific musical references.

2. Compare the sounds and textures heard in *Manteca* with those heard in *Tin Roof Blues*.

3. In what ways does 32-bar song form allow musicians more freedom than 12-bar blues? What alteration is made to standard 32-bar form in *Manteca*, and why?

---

## Miles Davis Quintet: *'Round Midnight*

Miles Davis (1926-1991) was one of the most influential jazz musicians in the second half of the 20th century. He made rapid progress on the trumpet and at the age of 18 left for New York, where he was soon working with his idols, Dizzy Gillespie and Charlie Parker.

The **bebop** style of trumpeter Gillespie and saxophonist Parker was fast and virtuosic. Although it was possible to dance to bebop, audiences tended not to. Bebop's hard-driven pace, dissonant harmonies and lack of easy melodies made it music for listening to rather than for dancing. Parker and his circle were happy to enjoy the intellectual status of being artists instead of entertainers, and took an interest in developments in classical music.

This is one of the three jazz recordings set for the exams in June 2015 and June 2016. Turn to page 144 for notes about exam questions on the jazz recordings.

By 1948 Davis was breaking away from Gillespie and Parker and beginning to form his own groups. He was dissatisfied with bebop as a style. Davis's own trumpet style was more economical than Gillespie's, less obviously bebop influenced. He preferred a middle-range sound to his mentor's 'screaming' register, with a controlled used of vibrato and a sensitive use of phrasing and silences. He often used pitch bends at the beginning and ends of notes, and

'*Round Midnight*, recorded 10 September 1956 in New York for Columbia Records.

| | |
|---|---|
| Trumpet: | Miles Davis |
| Tenor sax: | John Coltrane |
| Piano: | Red Garland |
| String bass: | Paul Chambers |
| Drums: | Philly Joe Jones |

demonstrated a flexible sense of timing, anticipating and delaying notes against the underlying pulse.

In the late 1940s Davis had set up a nonet (nine-piece band) with Canadian composer and arranger Gil Evans. They recorded some sessions that were eventually released in 1956 as the album *The Birth of the Cool*. This was heralded as a defining moment in the development of **cool jazz**, which was largely a reaction against the complexity of bebop and aimed to be easier on the ear, incorporating ideas from European classical music. However, Davis later distanced himself from the cool jazz style, and resented the fact that it was to some extent taken over by white jazz musicians such as Dave Brubeck.

Jazz pianist Thelonious Monk originally wrote the song '*Round Midnight* in 1940 or 1941. It quickly became the kind of ballad that jazz musicians of all styles wanted to play, Cootie Williams and Dizzy Gillespie being notable examples of those who made their own versions. Bernie Hanighen wrote some lyrics to go with the melody which became a favourite for vocalists too: listen to Ella Fitzgerald's recording as an example.

In 1955 Miles Davis made a guest appearance at the Newport Jazz Festival, and performed '*Round Midnight* with Thelonious Monk. His solo attracted a lot of attention, and many people saw it as a return to form for Davis, who had previously been fighting drug addiction. He was signed to Columbia Records on the strength of this performance, and created a new five-piece band to record the album that would become '*Round About Midnight*. This band became known as Miles Davis's 'first great quintet'.

By this time Davis's style had moved on from cool jazz. He wanted to recapture some of the excitement of bebop improvisations, and turn back to the African-American blues roots of jazz, away from the more Eurocentric tendencies of cool jazz. Davis released *Walkin'* in 1954, and this heralded the start of a new style, **hard bop**. *Walkin'* was written in 12-bar blues form, albeit an altogether more funky sort of blues than was previously usual, and had an earthy catchiness.

If you compare Davis's version of '*Round Midnight* with the other tracks on the same album, you will find that it does not share many characteristics with them. It is altogether softer in style, and is by far the slowest track on the album. However, it is testament to the fact that jazz musicians of all types love playing slow ballads, and '*Round Midnight* has a melody and harmonies that are enduringly popular.

## Structure

Miles Davis's version of *'Round Midnight* has the following structure:

| Introduction | 8 bars | 0:00-0:30 | Emphasis on trumpet |
|---|---|---|---|
| Chorus 1 | 32 bars | 0:30-2:39 | *aaba* song form, featuring trumpet |
| Interlude | 4 bars | 2:39-2:56 | A fanfare-like section |
| Chorus 2 | 32 bars | 2:56-5:07 | *aaba* song form, featuring tenor sax played by John Coltrane |
| Outro | 8 bars | 5:07 | Emphasis on trumpet |

Thelonious Monk's song is framed by the intro, interlude and outro, which Davis modelled in part on an earlier version of the song by Dizzy Gillespie.

## Introduction

The introduction, interlude and outro frame the two choruses, and are the only sections in which the whole band plays at once. Davis's muted trumpet plays a lazy, almost sequential melody for six bars:

> A mute is a device used to change the sound of an instrument. Trumpeters and trombonists have a huge range of mutes available, all of which are inserted into the bell of the instrument, and each gives a slightly different sound. They work by partially or completely blocking the air flow out of the bell, forcing some or all of the air through the mute. There are straight mutes, cup mutes, Harmon mutes and plunger mutes (among others), all of which are used to great effect by jazz musicians.

The mute he uses here is a stemless **Harmon mute**, which creates a slightly hard-edged, buzzing, yet intimate sound that became one of the Davis trademarks. The Harmon mute has a cork seal that forces all of the air through the instrument. The stem coming out of the middle can be adjusted to change the sound which is produced: Miles Davis removed the stem completely to create his signature sound. The rhythm here can be described as a **2-beat rhythm**, with the bass driving the harmonic rhythm with an emphasis on the first and third beats of the bar. At 0:24 the piano, bass and drums take over with an insistent rhythm:

This represents a very subtle introduction of a rhythmic feature known as **double-time**. This can be as simple as a doubling of the tempo in the rhythm section, used as a way of ramping up the energy levels. In *'Round Midnight* it is used in a much more unobtrusive way to add variety and a quiet injection of tension into the music. You can hear tiny versions of this idea in the second half of bar 2 and bar 4 of the introduction.

### Chorus 1 (trumpet)

Davis, continuing with his trademark muted sound, plays his version of Monk's melody, which is in conventional 32-bar song form. Again, there are small hints at double-time to give the rhythm a slight edginess, with the drums (played with brushes in this section) pulling against the mostly 2-beat feel of the bass at 1:32 and again at 2:10.

We hear an immensely subtle approach to rhythm here, with tiny variations being impossible to notate with absolute accuracy. With the rhythm section providing a rock-steady beat, Davis is able to pull the rhythm around with a huge amount of freedom, manipulating the length of notes and the way he attacks each one with infinite variety. It is impossible to say whether his rhythms are straight or swung, as often they are neither, or may change rapidly from one to the other.

The rhythm section continues with a straightforward 2-beat pattern until the *b* section of the song form, where the drums change to a double-time feel and the piano, having been playing two chords per bar previously, enjoys a slightly more active part. Philly Joe Jones plays a very simple rhythm using brushes on the snare, until the double-time passage, where he changes to a **shuffle** (swung) rhythm.

### The interlude

A lot happens in the four bars of the interlude. A bar of soft, quaver B♭s in octaves from the piano lulls the listener into a false sense of security before the whole ensemble plays a swinging, shouting repeated chord with the now unmuted trumpet in its highest register. This reaches a high E♭ (concert pitch D♭), which was right at the top of Davis's range. He uses the effort it clearly takes to play this note to create a contrast with the sound of his preceding muted solo. The rhythmic feel is now very much double-time. A very brief bass solo and drum roll – played here with sticks, not brushes – interrupt before another tutti scream leads into the tenor sax solo.

## Chorus 2 (tenor sax)

Here, the double-time feeling continues, but bass player Paul Chambers sticks to the patterns he played in Chorus 1, with bass notes mainly on the first and third beats. However, if you count this section at the original tempo, he is playing on every beat, making this a **4-beat** pattern. This ambiguity is part of the subtle charm and variety of this arrangement. The swing rhythms are now operating at a semiquaver, rather than quaver, level, and can therefore be described as **swing 16ths**. This has a lot more in common with the rest of the *'Round About Midnight* album, and with hard bop in general, than the earlier parts of the track.

John Coltrane has a much freer approach to the original melody of *'Round Midnight* than Miles Davis, quickly going off on a new path with his own melodic ideas. His characteristic sound has been described as 'steely', and the sometimes intense movement characteristic of his improvisations contrasted very effectively with Davis's feeling of space, as is shown to great effect on this track.

In this chorus, Philly Joe Jones continues using sticks, and his rhythm is a much more assertive shuffle beat featuring the ride cymbal and the closed hi-hat. Red Garland continues **comping** (playing rhythmic chords) but these are much more syncopated than in the first chorus. The bass plays mostly crotchets in a slow walking pattern, with the occasional more active flourish.

**Further reading**

*Miles Davis: The Definitive Biography* by Ian Carr. Harper Collins, 1982/1999. ISBN 978-0-006530-26-8. A fascinating account of Davis's life and music.

*It's About That Time: Miles Davis On and Off Record* by Richard Cook. Atlantic Books, 2005. ISBN 978-1-84354-332-9. An insightful guide to Davis's many recorded albums.

## Outro

The short outro serves to round off the piece by returning to the mood of the opening, with the trumpet taking the lead, although the saxophone does play a soft countermelody. Philly Joe Jones makes extensive use of the cymbals, including a cymbal roll at 5:09. The feel returns to 2-beat, with the bass and piano providing an uncluttered foundation for the rhythmic freedom of the front line.

### Exercise 35

1. What is hard bop? How is it different from bebop and cool jazz?

2. List the similarities and differences between the trumpet styles of Dizzy Gillespie and Miles Davis.

3. How did the life of a jazz musician change between the 1920s and the 1950s?

4. Compare the approaches in *Manteca* and *'Round Midnight* to (a) 32-bar song form, and (b) rhythm.

5. Explain the following terms: 2-beat, double-time.

## Questions on the jazz recordings

In Section B of the listening paper you will hear an extract from one of the three jazz recordings you have studied. You will be expected to be able to recognise which part of the complete recording it comes from and to answer a short series of questions worth 15 marks. These might ask you about:

➢ Who the performers are

➢ The performing techniques that they are using (such as the use of a mute or glissandi)

➢ When and where the recording was made.

Or you may be asked:

➢ To describe the music of a particular passage (such as the accompaniment or the use of a motif)

➢ To compare the chorus or a solo improvisation with one from elsewhere in the whole recording.

In Section C of the paper, which we look at in more detail in the next chapter, you might be asked:

➢ To compare the jazz styles used in two of the recordings you have studied

➢ To compare the role of an instrument in one of the three jazz recordings with the way a composer scored it in one of the three orchestral scores

➢ To place one of the jazz recordings in a historical context, or to compare its background with that of another jazz recording or orchestral score.

# Section C questions

For Section C of the paper you will have to write an essay – the only long piece of writing that you are asked to do for AS Music. You should take care over how you structure and express your answer because your quality of language will also be assessed.

You will have to answer **one** question from a choice of three. The questions will give you the opportunity to focus more closely on one or two of the six pieces you will have studied, but don't bank on your favourites coming up – you will have to be ready to write about any of them. Some questions might ask for a comparison between two of the pieces, perhaps about techniques of handling instruments, others might explore your knowledge of the context of one of them (explained below), or you may be asked about issues to do with reception, transmission or performance practice.

The better you know the music, the more convincing your answer is likely to be. Each time you make a general remark, such as how an instrument is used, you will make more of an impression on the examiner if you refer to precise examples from the piece concerned.

Your essay must answer the question set – irrelevant material, even if correct, is unlikely to receive credit. For example, if the question asks about Mozart's writing for strings, you will only waste time if you start by outlining the composer's life and works, or if you discuss other matters, such as form or tonality. Try to answer concisely and remember that you won't get marks for repeating points you have already made.

## Context

You will be expected to have developed a 'contextual awareness', that is an understanding of the broad background to the orchestral scores and jazz recordings that you have been studying; and your knowledge of any specific details that are known about the genesis of each piece – in other words, how it came into being. You need to know when and where the music was composed or first heard, and what sort of occasion it was for. For some pieces, little detail may be known, in which case you may have to focus on what concerts or recordings were usually like at the time.

Try to form a rough picture in your mind of places, types of building (venue) and audiences. What sort of people were they? Why had they come and what did they expect? Who were the musicians? How did they earn a living?

After closely studying the six pieces you should know quite a lot about the instruments and the ensembles involved. Compare the sort of orchestra used in Beethoven's Symphony No. 5 with Ellington's band for *Koko* or Dizzy Gillespie's for *Manteca*. How similar or different are the instruments and the ways in which they are combined? How has technology changed the sound that they make? How do the performing techniques differ?

## Essay-writing

The practice questions below will give you a good idea of the sort of essay you will be asked to write in the exam. Jot down half-a-dozen points about each of them as they occur to you and then practise your essay-writing technique by developing your notes into full answers for at least two of them. Remember that the way you express yourself and present your ideas will be assessed, so it is important to aim to be coherent and clear in the way you use words and shape sentences. Be careful about spelling: if you misspell the names of musicians or titles of pieces it will give a bad impression to the examiner.

Although there is a lot to do in the time, don't rush to spill everything you know about a particular piece down on the paper: take a few moments to think carefully about what the question is asking: what does the question expect you to do? Is it to compare, to describe, or to explain? Which pieces? How many of them? Which aspects? Make sure that what you write is really relevant: don't go into details of how bassoons are constructed if the question is about improvising techniques. Above all, the examiner wants to know how well you really know the music. The most convincing way to show this is by referring to an example – a melody, a riff, a chord, a rimshot – to illustrate the point in your answer. Be as precise as you can: explain exactly where in the music your example occurs, for instance 'the first trumpet riff can be heard at the start of the second chorus'.

## Further reading

You will probably have some favourites among the works you have been studying and might like to find out more about them. Or you may be asking some questions of your own – what did an early horn look like? How were early microphones different from those in use today? How did jazz spread beyond America? How is vibrato produced on a violin?

Depending on what you want to know, you may find the resources listed below helpful. The ultimate reference work for musicians is *The New Grove Dictionary of Music and Musicians* edited by Stanley Sadie and John Tyrrell (Oxford University Press, 2004, ISBN 978-0-195170-67-9). There is a separate *New Grove Dictionary of Jazz* by Barry Kernfeld (Oxford University Press, 2003, ISBN 978-1-561 592-84-5). Most major libraries have a reference copy and some allow borrowers to access the online version free of charge. However, it is extremely detailed and you may find that it tells you so much that it is difficult to get all the information straight in your head. The *Cambridge Music Guide* edited by Stanley Sadie and Alison Latham (Cambridge University Press, 1990, ISBN 978-0- 521399-42-5) is a useful and more manageable resource.

**Internet sites**  There is a wealth of information available on the internet, but remember that standards of accuracy and reliability vary. If you are a regular user of Wikipedia you will already know that while it is often a good starting point for research, the information there is not always correct in every detail. Some record companies put the sleeve notes from CDs on their websites and these can be a useful source of additional information.

Do remember that many music websites focus on biographical information about musicians, which will often not be relevant to your course. Try to use the web to answer questions about the music itself. Focus on the areas of study and building up your technical knowledge about the music you are studying.

The BBC Radio 3 website has useful information on both classical music and jazz. You can also listen to recent broadcasts online and follow links to other useful sites.

**Recordings**

It is advisable to study more than one recording of each of the set orchestral scores. For the set jazz repertoire it is essential to study the precise recordings listed on page 69. Don't forget that radio and TV are free sources of music: search the listings weekly, including channels that you don't normally turn to.

## Practice questions

1.  Discuss the principal differences between the orchestras of Handel and Beethoven, and how the composers wrote for them.

2.  Explain the circumstances in which **either** Handel composed the *Water Music* or Mozart composed the Horn Concerto No. 4 in E♭.

3.  If you were asked to prepare a performance of one of the prescribed orchestral works, what aspects would you need to consider? To what extent do you think it is important to respect the composer's intentions?

4.  Compare the way music was made available to audiences during 1920–1960 with the customs during the 18th and early 19th centuries. Refer in your answer to the background of one of the orchestral scores and one of the jazz recordings that you have studied.

5.  What similarities and differences were there between the working conditions of orchestral players in the 18th and early 19th centuries, compared to the jazz musicians in 1920–1960?

6.  Explain the role of Miles Davis as a soloist or band leader in **either** *Boplicity* **or** '*Round Midnight*.

7.  Explain which musical features of **either** Duke Ellington's *Koko* **or** Dizzy Gillespie's *Manteca* would have been familiar to audiences of the 1940s and which features would have been new.

8.  Describe the effect of radio and recording on the work of jazz musicians. Consider issues such as the advance of technology, the role of the radio and recording companies, the artistic and business opportunities presented by radio and recording, and the public response to broadcast and recorded performances.

9.  Compare how Handel or Beethoven used woodwind and brass instruments with the use of reeds and brass in one of the prescribed jazz recordings.

# Index

*page numbers in italics denote main entries*

# Acknowledgements

The authors and publisher are grateful to the following publishers for permission to use printed excerpts from their publications:

*The Pink Panther Theme*. Music by Henry Mancini. © Copyright 1964 Northridge Music Co. and EMI U Catalog Inc., USA. All Rights Reserved. International Copyright Secured.

*Hotter Than That*. Music by Lillian Hardin. © Copyright 1928 Universal/MCA Music Limited. All Rights Reserved. International Copyright Secured.

*Ko Ko*. Music by Edward Kennedy Ellington. © Copyright EMI Robbins Catalog Inc. EMI United Partnership Limited. All Rights Reserved. International Copyright Secured.

*Boplicity* (Be Bop Lives). Words & Music by Miles Davis & Gil Evans. © Copyright 1949 Jazz Horn Music Corporation, USA. Universal/MCA Music Limited/Copyright Control. All Rights Reserved. International Copyright Secured.

*Tin Roof Blues*. Words by Walter Melrose. Music by Paul Mares, Leon Rappolo, Ben Pollack, Melville Stitzel & George Brunies. © Copyright 1923 Herman Darewski Music Publishing Company/Redwood Music Limited. All Rights Reserved. International Copyright Secured.

*Manteca*. Words & Music by John Dizzy Gillespie, Gil Walter Fuller & Luciano Pozo Gonzales. © Copyright 1948 (Renewed) Music Sales Corporation (ASCAP)/Seemsa Sociedad Espanola De Ediciones Musical. All Rights Reserved. International Copyright Secured.

*Blue Moon*. Words by Lorenz Hart. Music by Richard Rodgers. © Copyright 1934 EMI-Robbins Catalog Inc. EMI United Partnership Limited. All Rights Reserved. International Copyright Secured.

*'Round Midnight*. Music by Cootie Williams & Thelonious Monk. © Copyright 1944 Advanced Music Corporation. Warner/Chappell Music Limited. All Rights Reserved. International Copyright Secured.

Page 80 photograph of Prince Frederick's Barge in the National Maritime Museum, Greenwich © Travel Pix Collection/AWL Images Ltd.